Sight-Fishing for

Striped Bass

Alan Caolo

Sight-Fishing for
Striped Bass

Alan Caolo
Cover Illustration Vaughn Cochran
Technique Illustrations Philip Caolo

Frank
Amato
PORTLAND

Published in 2001 by Frank Amato Publications, Inc.
P.O. Box 82112, Portland, Oregon 97282
(503) 653-8108 www.amatobooks.com

Softbound ISBN: 1-57188-253-7
Softbound UPC: 0-66066-00442-0
Hardbound ISBN: 1-57188-257-X
Hardbound UPC: 0-66066-00446-8

All photographs taken by the author unless otherwise noted.
Cover Illustration: Vaughn Cochran
Technique Illustrations: Philip Caolo
Book Design & Layout: Tony Amato

Printed in Singapore

3 5 7 9 10 8 6 4 2

CONTENTS

PREFACE 6
INTRODUCTION 8

1 SIGHT-FISHING WATERS 12

2 STRIPED BASS BEHAVIOR IN THE SIGHT-FISHING CONDITION ... 24

3 NATURALS 30

4 FLY PATTERNS FOR SIGHT-FISHING 38

5 SPOTTING THE FISH 46

6 PRESENTATION AND RETRIEVE 54

7 ANGLING STRATEGIES 64

8 TACKLE AND EQUIPMENT 80

9 SIGHT-FISHING DESTINATIONS 86

SUGGESTED READING AND VIEWING 99

Preface

Sight-fishing for striped bass is based on a fly fishing philosophy that was introduced by some of the most celebrated figures in saltwater angling. Thanks to the vision of Bill and Bonnie Smith, Joe Brooks, Capt. Jimmy Albright, A.J. McClane, and Stanley Babson, fly fishing the clear shallow flats was pioneered over fifty years ago. Much of *Sight-Fishing for Striped Bass'* content is broad-based and could serve as a primer for pursuing many flats game fish; including bonefish and permit. It would be personally irresponsible to not acknowledge that I have stood upon the shoulders of great sportsmen in preparing the first book devoted entirely to sight-fishing for stripers I also acknowledge the vision of Frank Amato, and I thank him for providing me the opportunity to pursue such a title. I am deeply thankful to Kim Koch, my friend and editor, for all that she's done to make this book all that it is. Tony Amato did an awesome job with the book's layout and I really appreciate his work. Captain Vaughn Cochran is an exceptional artist. *All* of his work is stunning and I'm thrilled he prepared the book's cover art. Thank you captain.

Sight-fishing for stripers is a relatively recent phenomenon. Having explored this fishery for several years, I realize that many progressive Northeast anglers mutually uncovered it with the striper's return around 1990. I acknowledge the efforts of Capt. Bob Benson, Capt. Rich Benson, Capt. Tony Biski, Capt. David Blinken, Capt. Paul Dixon, the late Capt. Paul Doyle, Lew Horton, Tim Leary, Capt. Jeff Northrop and George Ryan to bring the sport to where it is today.

Sight-Fishing for Striped Bass is based on my sight-fishing experiences over the last decade. I learned a great deal about fishing the Monomoy area from Capt. Kris Jop. Kris generously shared his knowledge with me and is a fine teacher. The book would not have been possible were it not for the support of *many* friends. I am deeply thankful to everyone who helped me.

To my brother, Philip Caolo, I am indebted. His painstakingly prepared illustrations are superb. They provide a clear picture of some not-so-clear concepts and add life to the text.

I worked with four photographers on this project, all of whom generously gave of their free time to help me. In particular, I owe a great deal of thanks to Darryl W. DeAngelis and Gail Letson for the many hours they patiently spent learning a sport they knew nothing about so as to photograph it accurately. The quality of their work stands out throughout the book in every photo that appears professional or otherwise the work of a trained eye; the other photographs are most likely mine. I thank Peter Jacobson and Dave Prigmore who, on a moment's notice, shot some fine action images. The aerial photography was made possible by the generous support of Harry Skinner, whose enthusiasm for flying made the "reconnaissance mission" thrilling as well as productive. Thanks Harry!

Six individuals made written contributions that add a regional flare to the text. I sincerely thank Capt. Andrew Cummings, Capt. Paul Dixon, Capt. Jeff Heyer, Capt. Kris Jop, Capt. Jeff Northrop, and Mr. Lou Tabory for taking time out of their very busy schedules to make this book better.

John Prigmore and the staff at Covedge Tackle were supportive in every way. Many of the flies and all of the nautical charts featured in the book were donated by Covedge. I appreciate John's generous support of this project.

Several of the featured fly patterns were developed by fine anglers. Johnny Glenn, Bob Popovics, Mark Lewchik, Ted Hendrickson, Tom Kintz, Kris Jop, John Prigmore and Dave Skok are innovative fly tiers that made contributions that are appreciated. My discussions with Page Rogers regarding the Martha's Vineyard fishery were informative. Many of her pattern creations are ideal for sight-fishing and are also featured in the book.

Cara Boland, Bob Froncillo and Liz McCusker are friends that provided me waterfront locations from which I could work effectively with cameras, fishing equipment, notepads, lenses and other tools of the trade.

The Electric Boat Corporation has been a gracious employer throughout my years as a fly fisherman. Their support allowed me the latitude necessary to finish the book. Short-notice vacations and the need to follow a flexible schedule from time to time while managing this endeavor were accommodated without question. I really appreciate it, EB.

Introduction

The diversity of our fly fishing world is expanding. Rapid technological development and hard work by innovative sportsmen over the last decade have provided fly fishers with a vast array of modern tackle, advanced techniques and worldwide angling opportunities. The most dramatic growth has been in salt water where changing attitudes on the part of sportsmen have led to unprecedented popularity in saltwater fly fishing.

The game fish sought by today's fly fisher are perhaps the best evidence of this growth. With the "bait and switch" technique and some very high-tech equipment nearly all the bluewater species are routinely taken now on fly gear. False albacore and bonito have become widely sought after inshore game fish albeit for decades only a few fly-rodding mavericks pursued them.

Exciting things are happening on the flats as well. Several innovative Northeast anglers and guides have begun exploring flats-fishing opportunities at home—*for striped bass*. Long thought to be exclusively a tropical experience, the successful introduction of southern-style flats-skiffs for stalking stripers on Northeast flats has proven otherwise. In a short time, fly-rodding for stripers has experienced a popular shift from traditional approaches. At the apex of the sport today is sight-fishing, where visual excitement and challenge provide fly-fishers a thrilling and rewarding angling experience.

Stripers are superb flats game fish and they're readily available to many fly-fishers. When striper stocks are up the sight-fishing opportunities are endless. When their numbers are down, sight-fishing is perhaps the most effective way of catching one on fly tackle. They offer a spectrum of challenge to suit the expectations of all fly fishers. The school-fish commonly associated with easy-to-fish inshore flats offer moderate challenge for beginners and casual sight-fishers. Experienced fly-fishers looking for a tougher challenge find the large, sophisticated fish on offshore flats more appealing. For anglers seeking trophy fish in a high-skill environment, the surf offers the "major league" experience. For some fly-fishers, sight-fishing is an exciting alternative during the hot summer months after the spring migration has evaporated and the fall migration is still months away. For others it is an obsession, where the fast action of spring and fall become the bookends to the preferred sight-fishing season. And for winter bonefish junkies in search of an off-season fix, stalking stripers in skinny water is a welcome surrogate. Stripers, however, are much closer to home for most of these folks, and no plane tickets or passports are required for a quick trip to the Northeast flats.

Visually stalking game fish with fly tackle is not new. Early fly-fishers began by casting dry flies to rising trout centuries ago, and the sport remains as challenging and as popular today. In salt water, anglers have been sight-fishing for bonefish, tarpon, and permit for decades and the immense popularity of this sport has ignited an entire industry throughout the tropics. In light of the challenges involved and the potentially overwhelming complications of adverse weather, third-world destinations, Miami International, hostile natives, sharks, toxic sea-life, and more, it may seem puzzling that anglers the world over ardently pursue this brand of fly fishing (at great expense, mind you).

To pinpoint sight-fishing's vast appeal is difficult. *Visual excitement, mental absorption* and *challenge* immediately come to mind—but it may be more than that. Most game fish we stalk on the flats may be pursued in other ways. Look at the addiction we call bonefishing. *Albula vulpes* can easily be taken off the flats in deep water with some ground shrimp and a little patience. Even a blind-folded first-timer can catch a trophy bone this way. But very few people do it, and fly-fishers don't even consider it. Sight-casting to the Silver King is even more confounding. Talk about a low percentage endeavor! Yet, countless tarpon skiffs dot the Florida Keys' horizon each spring with anxious anglers vying for the thrill of casting to those magnificent fish.

Sight-fishing appeals to many anglers simply because everything that takes place between you and your quarry is witnessed. Somewhat of a double-edged sword, this can be a euphoric angling triumph, or a frustrating bout of rejection. How easy it is while blind-casting to presume that there are no fish where you are when the strikes do not come. It is indeed the rare angler who remains objective and assumes nothing in these circumstances. Sight-casting, on the other hand, provides the luxury of knowing this part of the puzzle without doubt. It also provides you the knowledge that you've done everything right, or that you have not.

Less obvious is the combination of primordial instincts to fish and hunt, which is so perfectly provided with sight-fishing. Such a combination preoccupies the mind to produce a focused and continuous involvement. Even when the fish are not cruising in your view and your fly is still in hand—*you are stalking them*, and opportunity may prevail at any moment. Presenting to a mere 10 fish throughout a three-hour span is easily perceived as solid action.

The intensity and excitement of this sport is thrilling. While sight-fishing, anglers encounter their quarry on its terms, and they must perform on cue. This is challenging fishing, and casting skills must be above average. Unlike blind-casting, sight-casting offers little choice as to cast direction, distance, and timing. Consistently successful sight-fishers are above all else, calm and competent fly-casters.

Competent casting is consistently accurate, smooth, long when necessary, immune to adverse wind direction, and is only achieved through practice. Calm fly-casting is the ability to continue casting competently when the fish are in sight. Since the fish usually appear suddenly and are often moving quickly, the excitement can cause many sight-fishers to react frantically and fail to make a good cast. Staying calm when a trophy striper appears in your casting range is not easy, but it is a skill that must be developed to make the most of the opportunities you work to create. As with tarpon and bonefish, calm casting is acquired through experience. Even the veterans get excited with the sight of a great game fish on the flats. It wouldn't be much fun if you didn't. They stay cool, however, and make the cast that gets the fish. Only saltwater sight-fishing offers this angling intensity and excitement.

Much like bonefishing, consistent success with stripers on the flats comes to those who pay attention to detail. There are no "magic dart" flies; there is just doing as many little things right as often as you can. That is the challenge. The ability to see everything that takes place—the fish's movements, its reaction to the fly, a follow, a refusal, or a take, are not only exciting to witness, but the analysis of these observations and subsequent adjustment on your part are at the heart of the sport. The ultimate solid hookup is thrilling, as it is head-shaking, reel-screaming proof that you have done *everything* right. You should rightly feel proud of every striper hooked while sight-fishing. Each one is an accomplishment. Most veteran sight-fishers insist they would rather take one bass by sight than 10 or 15 any other way. How do I feel about it? I rarely fish blind for them any more.

Perhaps the most interesting aspect of the sport pertains to the fish itself. Many anglers become fascinated with a striped bass they have never seen before. Quite unlike the aggressive nocturnal feeder, so readily taken in twilight hours, deep waters, and during migration, stripers are casual and comfortable as they graze the shallows by day. Unlike tropical flats species, stripers *are* the top of the food chain while on the flats. Demonstrating a true intelligence and a capacity to remember, striper behavior is wildly more interesting (and far less predictable) than that of other Northeast game fish. The secret life of this remarkable creature is starkly revealed to those who pursue them by sight.

I believe this behavior is rooted in the striped bass' evolutionary past. With an entire life cycle that spans a mere few miles off the mainland to several miles inland through estuary and river systems, the striper's domain fully overlaps with the human existence. Their Atlantic range is domestic when compared to that of the globally distributed bonefish or the pelagic nomads. The process of natural selection has perfected the striper for an entirely coastal existence *and* an innate ability to coexist with Man and human activity.

These factors have produced a fascinating flats game fish that can get in an angler's mind like no other species we fish for. Although always challenging, stripers on the flats are readily taken with the right approach. In the chapters that follow, I share the details of what I've learned in a decade of sight-fishing—what the sport is all about, when, where, and why it occurs, and how to approach it with the right attitude to consistently succeed.

Chapters One and Two describe sight-fishing waters and the striper's unique behavior as he roams these clear, shallow

flats in search of food during the warm months of June, July, August and September. Understanding striper behavior while up on bright flats is central to formulating an angling strategy, selecting a fly and making your presentation. The ability to recognize a quality sight-fishing flat is important and it will save you time when exploring new locations. This knowledge is the key to discovering new sight-fishing opportunities—sometimes where you least expect them.

Stripers are drawn to the shallows to feed on unique forage that is indigenous to these waters in the summer months. Northeast fly fishers are familiar with most of these naturals, but some may surprise you. Knowledge of these food sources is vital to your success and Chapter Three is devoted to the subject. Effective sight-fishing fly patterns that imitate these prey are covered in Chapter Four.

The art of spotting fish is covered in Chapter Five. Your success while sight-fishing is directly proportional to how well you see the fish—the more stripers you're able to spot, and the quicker you see them, increases the number of presentations you'll make and ultimately how many stripers you will hook.

The technical aspects of the sport are discussed in Chapter Six, "Presentation and Retrieve". A calm and controlled approach, as opposed to frantically tossing your fly anywhere out in front of moving fish is essential to consistent success. Five basic presentations and how to use them on inshore flats, offshore flats, and the surf are discussed. Three advanced presentations for dealing with difficult circumstances are also covered.

Angling strategy is important when sight-fishing for any game fish. With stripers, your success depends on it. From a broad perspective, the sport may be pursued in three distinct arenas: wading inshore flats, working offshore flats by boat, and sight-fishing the surf. Successful strategies for these different waters are described in Chapter Seven. This chapter draws on material covered in the previous chapters and ties it all together to guide the reader, as though actually on the flats.

A tackle chapter is included to share my experience on what works best and why. There's nothing exotic here, just some tips and tricks on how to best rig and use the equipment you probably already own.

Sight-fishing is available throughout the striper's migratory range, whenever the conditions are right. In the Northeast, this occurs during the summer from northern New Jersey to southern Maine. Seven prominent sight-fishing locations are highlighted in the final chapter, entitled "Sight-Fishing Destinations". This information comes to you courtesy of some of the most generous and knowledgeable people in the sport. Less dramatic, but still high quality sight-fishing is common throughout the Northeast on a smaller scale. Modestly proportioned flats throughout Long Island and New England offer numerous opportunities. These less conspicuous flats, typical of the Rhode Island and Martha's Vineyard fisheries, probably surpass all the major destinations combined in aggregate acreage. The availability of these small flats is part of the reason why striper sight-fishing is a treasure—it's literally in our backyards.

The growing interest in sight-fishing for striped bass is a striking example of how our sport is evolving. As the author of this book, my goal is to bring fellow fly-fishers up to date on this exciting new sport. I guarantee that sight-fishing for stripers will enrich your fly-fishing world.

Chapter 1
Sight-Fishing Waters

The first step when sight-fishing is to find suitable waters in which to stalk stripers. Quality flats have certain geologic and marine characteristics that ensure consistent water clarity, support a healthy, nutrient-rich bottom, moderate water temperatures, and consistently draw stripers to feed. The layout of the bottom contour, including shoals, drop-offs, channels, sand bars, holes and the accessibility to and from deep water that stripers use to enter and exit the flats, strongly influences how well a flat will fish.

If you fish with a guide you should hire someone who specializes in sight-fishing. Sight-fishing guides know where and when to find the fish, they know how to stalk them and they will be properly equipped. When fishing on your own, suitable flats may be located by field observation (during both low and high tides), examining nautical charts and coastal maps, and by aerial inspection, if that's realistic for you. Getting up in a small aircraft over waters you plan to fish often is an invaluable experience and it's not expensive if a few friends get together and hire a pilot for an afternoon; don't forget the camera. Talk to people involved around the water whenever you can. Surfers, jet skiers (here's your chance to make something positive of them), swimmers and clam diggers are all reliable spotters and most know a striper when they see one. Unlike other anglers, who may be reluctant to pass this information on, these folks are usually more than happy to help.

All flats are not necessarily good sight-fishing waters. Some shallow areas are great for evening fishing but attract few fish during the day. Others may hold fish only during specific seasonal events, such as annual worm hatches. Still others may be fertile areas, but have dark or weed-covered bottoms that make spotting fish difficult. And some are just plain inert and do not attract stripers, period. Sight-fishing flats have distinct features that differentiate them from other inshore waters. Knowing these attributes enables you to consistently locate probable flats on which to find cruising bass.

The most important element is a rich food supply. Without it, a flat becomes a very unlikely sight-fishing area. The *variety* of prey governs how well the flat will continue to fish as the striper's food preference shifts throughout the season. For example, inshore stripers may feed steadily on juvenile sand eels and flounder for four or five weeks and then leave the estuary with the seaward departure of these baitfish in early summer. Strong resident shrimp and crab populations, however, will hold these fish whose dietary preference simply shifts to a new food source.

— Inshore Flats —

Of the three sight-fishing environments, inshore flats are the most prevalent and generally the easiest to access. The combination of marine and geographic ingredients required to produce quality fishing come together far more often than those required for sight-fishing beaches and there is no need for a skiff. The countless small- and medium-sized inshore flats scattered throughout the Northeast certainly surpass all the marquis offshore destinations combined in total aggregate acreage. These flats are found along harbor and bay edges, inside protected barrier beaches, and throughout salt ponds and estuary systems. Flats surrounded by tidal marshland are particularly fertile, sustaining a wide variety of prey and consistent sight-fishing throughout the season. Their diverse structure creates a multitude of interesting opportunities for the sight-

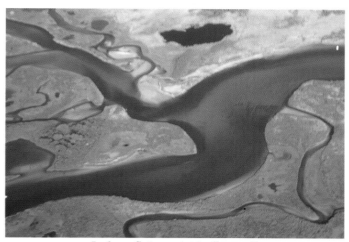

Inshore flats are typically small, intricate areas that are fished surgically.

fisher and the same skills and thought process that go into reading bonefish flats apply here. It is here that sight-fishing for stripers and bonefishing become nearly the same.

Inshore flats are most effectively fished by walking the water's edge or by wading in knee-deep water. The fishing is more intimate than the big-water, team operation typical of the offshore experience, and it is far more tranquil than the exhilarating, high-energy experience of the surf. The fish most often found in these waters run smaller than those normally found on ocean flats and are noticeably less educated. As a result, inshore fishing is simpler than in other sight-fishing waters. Forgiving fish in a forgiving fly fishing environment moderate the challenge making this the best place to learn and gain experience. It's fun and relaxing fishing—no boat, no guide, no waves, plenty of space and plenty of hungry fish!

These are protected waters that have distinct advantages and disadvantages relative to offshore and surf areas. They are immune to surf condition and much less prone to the high winds common on offshore flats. When a source of clear, clean ocean water for tidal flushing is nearby, their water clarity will be consistently good. On the other hand, too much isolation can make inshore flats prone to high water temperatures in midsummer, especially in the southern part of the sight-fishing range where warm ocean water may not cool the flats sufficiently to sustain striper activity.

The sand or mud flats associated with many inshore waters become fully exposed at low tide (this occurs on some flats only during full and new moon lunar phases when tidal range is maximal). Here, the timing of tides, the availability of sunlight and water temperatures must be juggled to define windows of opportunity when everything comes together to produce good fishing; much like bonefishing. For example, a morning outgoing tide at the height of summer usually flows cool with good water depth, and generally yields good fishing. During the day the water warms and fishing tapers off somewhat. The afternoon incoming tide again floods the flats with cool ocean water producing good fishing later in the day. On the other hand, a morning incoming tide produces good water

depth and moderate water temperature for only a few hours around mid-day. The warm water and diminishing depths associated with the afternoon outgoing tide often produces weak results.

The best time for fishing inshore waters occurs within the striper's non-migration period where the fish you spot are often members of large, resident schools. Here lies the main difference between inshore and offshore areas. Inshore flats experience their best sight-fishing during the non-migration period from June through August with resident fish that remain for the abundance of prey found there in the summer. Offshore flats, on the other hand, experience their best sight-fishing during the peaks of the spring and fall runs, with a lull period in midsummer.

Proximity to Deep Water and Tidal Flushing

Inshore waters are protected from the direct effects of ocean winds and waves making them placid and consistently fishable, but they still must have good contact with the sea. Productive flats are situated relatively near the ocean and experience a healthy exchange of seawater during each tide cycle. Inlets, harbor entrances and river mouths in direct contact with sounds and the ocean itself all provide good sources of water for nearby flats with every incoming tide. Tidal flushing regulates temperature, flushes biological waste, replenishes oxygen levels, and preserves high water clarity. All of these factors are vital to maintaining a large biomass of forage that attracts stripers to feed.

Inshore areas too isolated from the sea, such as the far reaches of coastal rivers or complex estuary systems, do not receive adequate tidal flushing and often suffer from excessive water temperatures. Brackish water river systems tend to be tannic or tea-colored and seldom have the light sand bottom required for spotting. The flats found throughout well-flushed estuaries and which line the edges of harbors and deep-water bays are generally good bets.

Drop-offs, sandbars, channels and proximity to the open sea via inlets enhance the sight-fishing on inshore flats.

Sight-fishing on inshore flats is regulated by tides. Much like bonefishing, many flats are simply too shallow at low tide for the fish to embark the flat and feed; others become fully high and dry. Some flats are fishable during any stage of the tide, but they are less common. The fishing must be planned around the tides to ensure that the conditions will be right. Some areas fish best with an incoming tide while others during the outgoing. This must be determined through time spent on the water, or by fishing with a local guide. Either way, knowledge of the tide schedule, based on either a local tide table or the moon phase, is imperative when planning a trip.

Tides influence water temperature during the course of the day. Fishing is often planned around optimum water temperature, which is controlled by sunlight, tides and overnight cooling effects—especially late in the season when the waters have warmed considerably. Surface waters cool considerably during clear nights (radiant cooling). Shallow flats are cooled substantially overnight with clear skies, sometimes as much as 10 degrees F, which often produces good fishing in the morning when the tide is up. However, if the tide is high at mid-day, the outgoing water in the afternoon may have warmed too much during the day and fishing may be slow until the next incoming tide cools the sun-baked flats. No computer program has yet to be devised that can precisely predict these day-to day phenomena with much consistency (nor would such a tool be much fun anyway) so anglers must analyze conditions as they unfold. Knowing the basic effects of tides, sun and radiant cooling on water temperature is valuable when fishing inshore flats. A water thermometer is helpful for assessing these issues. In general, striper activity drops off progressively as the water temperature moves beyond the 72-degree mark.

Bottom Types: Sand, Mud and Shell

Inshore flats have various bottom types, including sand, mud, rock, grass and shell. All of them are capable of sustaining healthy supplies of prey, but for sight-fishing, the light background of sand and shell bottoms are ideal. The fine texture of sand holds all manner of burrowing prey that draw stripers. Shell bottoms consist of uniformly scattered, broken shells (usually clam shells) that rest on top of sand or mud bottoms. The bright reflection from the white shells creates a dramatic background for spotting fish and the nooks and crannies formed by the broken shells are an attractive habitat for shrimp, crabs and small baitfish. Mud and grass bottoms are ideal feeding areas for bass, but their dark color makes spotting difficult and their soft sediments are often unpleasant to wade. Rock bottoms hold plenty of forage too, but again spotting can be difficult here with the exception of first light, when stripers often appear pale blue over the rocks.

The most productive inshore flats have eelgrass beds as part of their composition. These may be small patches that dot the sand flats, or they may be wide areas that flank or surround the flats. Either way, they are ideal habitat for crabs, shrimp and baitfish. Stripers use them extensively for feeding and as holding areas when they are inactive. Much of the prey that stripers pursue on the flats is supported by the oxygen and nutrients provided by such marine vegetation.

Bass frequently work the edges of sharp, highly visible drop-offs.

Sandbars, Channels and Drop-Offs

Inshore flats are composed of a variety of fishing structure. Most significant are sandbars, channels and drop-offs, which control the flow of water to and from the flats and influence the movements of stripers and prey. These features are important to sight-fishers for locating fish and formulating strategies for stalking them. Cautious stripers will generally not embark a flat during the day without a nearby presence of deep water for a safe escape, regardless of the amount of food it harbors.

Channels may run as slight depressions a few feet deeper than the surrounding water, or they may be several feet deep where the bottom is no longer visible. Either way, they serve as a primary conduit for transporting water to and from the flats. The water in them obviously flows deeper than the surrounding water and it is also cooler (especially near the bottom). Both of these effects make channels ideal passages for stripers to inconspicuously navigate the area. When feeding conditions are right, stripers leave the channels and cruise the flats for prey. Stripers often hold in shallow channel currents, which they use as feeding lanes. These channels are ideal places for anglers look for holding fish or post-up and intercept transiting fish.

Drop-offs are sudden transitions from shallow flat to deep water that may run for several hundred yards, defining the edge of the flat. Generally they are visibly well defined. The deeper waters off these edges are cool, comfortable places for stripers to hold or feed when conditions are not right on the flats. But when water depth and temperature conditions become suitable, stripers will pour out of these drop-offs and onto the flats for feeding. Stripers also like to cruise these edges during low tide, making them prime locations for post-up fishing. As with channels, drop-offs make stripers comfortable by providing a ready deep-water escape route off the flats.

Sandbars are fine-sand formations that are created and shaped by wind and current effects. The flats themselves are nothing more than very large sandbars. Most bars are not well

Estuaries are fertile areas that support superb sight-fishing.

defined in shape and they are best observed, or "read", at low tide when they are exposed. They consist of shifting sands that may be considerably reconfigured, or washed out altogether, in the course of a season or two. They significantly affect currents and prey movement, both important when sight-fishing. Currents move fast around the edges and over the tops of shallow sandbars, often sweeping baitfish with them. By collecting sand, sandbars also collect larvae of crabs, shrimp and worms, creating localized, hot feeding areas for stripers.

Estuaries, Marshes, and Shoreline Structure: the Nursery

Inshore flats are found in conjunction with a variety of marine shorelines, but the most productive flats are associated with estuaries. Here, adjacent marshlands and tide-pools serve as rich breeding areas for many forms of marine wildlife. These marshes are infused with surrounding tidal waters through narrow natural and man-made waterways, forming the estuary.

Deep grass banks attract crabs, baitfish and daytime-feeding stripers.

These estuarine networks are perfect biological habitats for spawning and they serve as the nursery for countless marine organisms, many of which are prey relished by striped bass. The overall system of wetlands, marsh banks and protected shallow flats support a wide variety of prey all season long, making estuaries premium sight-fishing choices.

Estuaries are usually lined with deep grass banks that provide further protection for prey along the main body of water. Crabs and baitfish rely on these banks for cover and frequently stay very close to them during the day, especially during high tide when stripers can prowl right up to the water's edge. Anglers can take advantage of these elevated banks, which form ideal vantage points for spotting fish and making presentations. Again, this is especially true during high tide when stripers are able to reach the shoreline, where they love to feed. Shorelines consisting of a series of points and coves are attractive to fish and fishermen. Small coves that lie between shoreline points are out of the main current and often hold pockets of prey seeking their protection and warm water. When the tide is high enough, stripers cruise these coves for easy feeding.

Human Activity

In contrast to the surf, where stripers quickly become tolerant of human presence, the fishing on inshore flats can be adversely affected by human activity. These areas are suitable for clamming, boating, wind surfing, jet skiing and more. As a result, the activities of other people must often be factored into your angling strategy. It's a relative thing; a quiet kayaker will probably spook few fish, unless he or she glides right over them. Half-dozen youngsters running across a flat, on the other hand, will surely put the bass off for quite a while. Most times these people have no idea what flats anglers are doing. They cannot possibly imagine how or why you would attempt to catch a fish in such shallow water and they often try to help you by advising where to find water nearby that's ". . . over your head."

Fishing an entirely unoccupied flat is of course ideal, however, that is sometimes difficult in many popular Northeast areas during the summer. I find that politely approaching others enjoying the outdoors near the flat you intend to fish and explaining what you're doing to them and why that piece of water is so important to you prevents a lot of frustration and conflict later on. Most times these folks don't care where they run their jet skies or run with the dog and they gladly give you your space. Clam diggers, on the other hand, operate quietly and they often attract hungry bass with the bottom-prey they stir up. It always pays to look carefully in the down-tide mud of clam diggers.

— Offshore Flats —

Offshore sight-fishing is often compared to flats fishing in tropical locations, such as the Florida Keys. As their name implies, these flats are located some distance off shore and must be accessed by boat. Once anglers have reached the fishing grounds they may fish them from the skiff, to cover large areas, or disembark to stalk specific areas on foot.

The flats off Sandy Point, Rhode Island are typical of mid-sized offshore flats.

In addition to mobility, fishing from a skiff has other advantages. Anglers achieve enhanced viewing while standing several feet above the water on the skiff's casting deck. They also benefit from an experienced guide, whose trained

Fishing from the skiff offers better spotting and greater mobility when fishing these large areas.

eyes are even higher above water when the boat is equipped with a poling platform. Hence, fishing from the skiff is generally the best option when working waters over two feet deep, or to improve spotting when the viewing is marginal. Wading is most effective in waters less than two feet deep where the skiff's presence may alert stripers and put them off the feed.

Offshore areas are best fished with an experienced sight-fishing guide who knows the waters. Guides know the fish and their habits, what flies are hot, and where to be on these huge flats at any given time to provide you the best opportunities on a given day. There are several first-class sight-fishing guides available in most regions that sport a sight-fishery and I highly recommend utilizing these professionals. A good guide is a good teacher and coach from whom you can learn a lot in a day.

These areas should be attempted on your own only after the area has been carefully surveyed. This is accomplished by reviewing nautical charts, NOAA current charts (if available) and speaking with locals to get a feel for the waters. On many flats the outgoing tide can easily leave a skiff high and dry if you're careless. Be aware of all hazards that can damage or strand boats venturing into these areas—before you set out. Unless you're operating a safe vessel that meets all U.S. Coast

Guard rules and regulations for inshore craft and draws 18 inches of water or less, you shouldn't consider going on your own.

Offshore flats often lie within migratory routes that striped bass follow as they travel northward in the spring and southward in the fall. As a result, large numbers of fish are consistently seen transiting these flats each year. Encountering large striper schools containing hundreds and even thousands of fish on any given day is typical here during the early and late fringes of the season (May/June and September/October). Numerous pods of trophy fish, numbering 10 to 50 fish in a school, also pass through at these times. In May and June the fish are fresh off the spring migration and offshore waters are still relatively cool. These early-season stripers feed more actively and respond aggressively to flies. As waters warm later on, the fish settle down and become noticeably selective, less aggressive feeders.

These flats are generously swept with clean, clear ocean water, which supports a healthy, stable food chain. Abundant food sources, consisting of year-round resident prey within the bottom and seasonal baitfish schools, hold large numbers of migrating stripers for days or weeks at a time for interim feeding. As a result, offshore flats consistently produce outstanding sight-fishing opportunities making the extra effort required to get to them well worth it.

Water Cleanliness and Temperature

In contrast to inshore flats, offshore areas are fully immersed in the open ocean. The flushing these areas receive with every tide cycle ensures top-quality water conditions throughout the season (the exceptions being the extremes of hurricane or tropical storm events). Large quantities of forage are sustained by cool waters and continuous biological waste removal provided by direct tidal exchange with the open ocean. Consistently high visibility and moderate water temperatures prevail throughout the season as well, keeping the fish active and ensuring a dependable, often spectacular sight-fishing experience here.

Bottom Type

Most productive flats consist of white-sand bottoms. With good viewing, the fish are easily spotted over these pale backgrounds, allowing the long presentations often called for. Fine-textured sand is ideal for harboring bottom-dwelling prey and it lends itself to the formation of sandbars, a very important element of offshore flats structure.

Many offshore areas are enriched with lush eelgrass beds, which are excellent habitat for supporting many prey species. Striped bass feed in these beds, and hold in them for cover when they are not feeding. Flats augmented with grass generally hold more migrating stripers for longer periods than those without grass. Stripers are often spotted cruising grass bed edges while feeding, many times in large schools. These edges are ideal spots to stake-out and intercept these fish.

Offshore flats may have large clam beds as part of their ecosystem. While not directly visible, these rich areas are revealed by clam diggers that work them with bull rakes. The clams themselves are not a common food source for stripers, but the sea worms also found in these clam beds are. Bass devour these worms when they are unearthed by clam diggers, or by natural events such as storms. Clam-bed locations should always be considered when formulating an offshore strategy.

Islands, Shoals, Sandbars and Channels

Many features associated with offshore flats are similar to those found on inshore waters. However, the better visibility resulting from the skiff's higher elevation allows deeper channels and shoal edges to be sight-fished here, while on inshore flats they cannot. Offshore channels are not as important for supplying ocean water to the flats, nor are they as important for striper access since the ocean surrounds these areas. Nevertheless, stripers do transit them and they become main arteries during low-tide periods.

Sandbars are important to the overall ecology of an offshore flat. They direct water flows on and off the flats, support bottom-dwelling food sources (including clams, worms and crabs), and they're often part of the sight-fishing strategy. Sandbars consist of fine sands that constantly shift with wind- and tide-generated currents. Sandbars continuously change their shape, depth and location as a result. Knowing where such shifts have occurred is important when planning an angling strategy and for boating safety.

Sandbars hold prey and influence currents over the flats. They are widely used by sight-fishers to intercept stripers feeding and travelling in these currents. The flow of water downstream of sandbars is often turbulent, making an ideal location for stripers to catch bait as it is swept with the tide. Shoals are similar to sandbars in their effect, however, they are rigidly composed, stationary features.

Many offshore waters are bordered by neighboring islands. Islands make great weather-breaks, and the lee side can be a comfortable place to fish when the wind is up. With

Deep channels, such as this one at Monomoy, are transited by stripers and provide excellent edges for stalking bass.

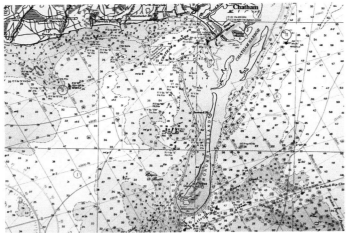

Many offshore flats are protected by barrier islands and shoals.

✦ ⊱✦⊰ ✦

the reduced chop in the lee, the water remains clear and the visibility good even when the wind has been blowing for several days. Islands also behave like enormous sandbars and direct the flow of water, bait and striped bass. Bass frequently feed adjacent to islands, working parallel to the shore in large schools. Island shorelines, like the mainland, provide excellent habitat for prey and are perfect places for stripers to feed.

Tides

Water level and current fluctuate over all flats in response to the tides. A complete tide cycle is about 12 hours on average—six hours flooding in to high tide, followed by six hours flowing out to low tide, and then all over again. Tides are caused by the effects of the moon's gravitational pull on the oceans that cover the earth, which create a slight bulge in the liquid surface that propagates over the earth's surface as our planet spins on its axis.

The range of water level fluctuation and the duration of each tide cycle vary throughout the month as the moon's

✦ ⊱✦⊰ ✦

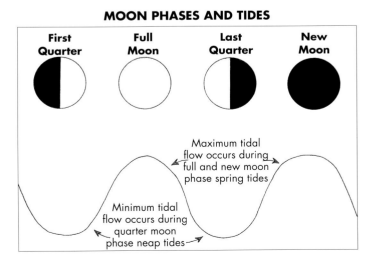

pull waxes and wanes along with the lunar cycle. Tidal range between high and low tide is greatest when the sun and moon are on opposite sides of the earth in what we commonly recognize as full and new moon phases. The resulting tides are referred to as "spring tides" with flow rates and water levels significantly greater than normal. Minimal range occurs during the quarter moon phases in between, with what are known as "neap tides". Tidal range also varies with latitude. In the southern end of the sight-fishing range this is about three feet between high and low tide. On Cape Cod and north of Boston this can be as much as seven feet.

Valid computer models or local tide charts yield very accurate tide predictions. Without these tools, however, tide schedules may be approximated by noting the phase of the moon. For example, high tide will prevail at about the same times of day in a given area during each specific moon phase. New moon, first quarter, full moon and last quarter lunar phases regulate the tides and produce similar schedules from month to month. Once you know these for a given area you can pretty much do away with tide tables and use any calendar that indicates moon phase instead. Or simply look at the evening sky.

Tides are somewhat influenced by wind, which can push the tide in sooner than expected or hold water levels higher than expected for longer periods when the wind opposes the direction of the tide, thus delaying the outgoing tide. Wind-induced tidal variation is generally insignificant at wind velocities below 10 knots, but it becomes increasingly significant at higher velocities. The effects of significant winds and marine storms must always be considered when figuring tides by adding or subtracting minutes to scheduled predictions.

Offshore striper activity is largely governed by tides. The fish generally move on and off the flats swimming with or against the flow of water, and adequate water level may not be present in some areas until the tide has come in for an hour, or more. Just as important, certain areas may be accessible with a skiff only during higher stages of the tide. This can dictate when you're able to get to these flats, as well as when you should leave (lest you wait several hours for the tide to bring the water level back up). Baitfish transiting offshore flats are swept with the tide as they migrate through, which can influence the where-abouts of stripers. Clams are dug commercially on many flats, which stirs bottom sediments and unearths prey. These are carried in a predictable direction off the flats during the outgoing tide. Anglers may capitalize on this phenomenon by intercepting hungry fish following the trail to its source.

Water flow on and off large offshore flats is uniform to an extent, however, the water flowing through channels running to or from adjacent deep water still predominate. These arteries experience significant tidal flow for longer periods and, in general, experience greater numbers of forage and game fish passage than areas with less flow. This is significant for several reasons. First, stripers like most game fish, feed very little during non-flow tidal stages, known as "slack tide". Areas with prolonged tide flow, on the other hand, offer longer periods of striper fishing.

Second, stripers are casual and selective while grazing the flats. The slower the current is flowing, the more time they have to mull over whether or not to take a fly, which is one reason why sight-fishing is a challenge in the first place. Unlike the fast waters of rips and rivers that force fish to capture prey quickly, shallow flats offer the fish more time to examine an offering, and they can become picky. Periods of peak water velocity during maximum tide flow become significant on some flats as the fish have less time to react to prey, often causing them to feed more aggressively. This fact makes fishing through these periods simpler in that the fish are more easily fooled with less exact patterns and less precise presentations; *the fishing gets easier.* Areas where the tide runs strong for long periods are advantageous for obvious reasons. Peak tide flow generally prevails during the second and third hours of the tide. Water temperatures are also moderated (cooled) during peak tidal flow, which can trigger stripers to become more aggressive.

And third, many fish, including stripers, relocate between feeding areas or otherwise change their position during slack tide. On offshore flats, where the fish often transit long distance over shallow water (instead of deep channels and drop-offs as on inshore flats), relocating, non-feeding fish are often spotted by anglers who attempt catching them where there is inherently little hope. Similar to trying for sated bonefish anxious to exit the flats near the end of the outgoing tide. Continuing to stalk fish *where water movement remains strongest* as the tide slows often proves more successful on offshore flats.

— The Surf —

Sight-fishing beaches are spectacular. They come in many sizes but most often they are long—interlocking land and sea for miles with restless surf. The surf is unquestionably the most challenging environment in which to sight-fish. It is also the most exciting and a consistent producer of trophy stripers.

Sight-fishing beaches are perfect for wade-fishermen. Their direct contact with the open sea ensures surf, clean water and an intertidal zone, all key elements for making them productive sight-fishing beaches. Working from a skiff here is both ineffective and unsafe. Wading is the only way to effectively stalk your quarry and maneuver in this dynamic environment while making complex presentations to fast-moving targets.

The surf is an exhilarating, high-skill environment for sight-fishers. This is perhaps the most athletic fly-fishing there is. Fishing the surf often calls for miles of brisk wading, both out of the water in soft sand and in knee-deep wash. Occasionally, anglers may remain stationary for long periods by posting-up, but more often they burn calories and they're not afraid to get wet. Unlike other sight-fishing waters, anglers frequently spot fish well beyond casting range and are able to successively reposition themselves for several presentations to the same fish.

The surf is by far the most sensitive sight-fishing environment to adverse natural and human influences. In addition to the usual factors of wind, sun and water clarity, beaches are also at the mercy of the open sea through incoming waves and by widespread human activity. The pristine features that make a beach a sight-fishing beach are the same ingredients that make these shorelines ideal for beach-goers of all sorts. If the surf has a pitfall it is its vulnerability to the ocean, weather and excessive human activity.

Bathers are usually unaware of the stripers around them, which often feed around their legs and feet. These swimmers are understandably not fond of hooked lures being cast in their direction and hence they pose an obstacle for fly-fishers. A continuous stream of pedestrians along the water's edge adds yet another variable that anglers must remain aware of as far as the backcast is concerned. Sight-fishing on popular beaches at the height of the season may be more bother than it's worth, especially on beaches that cater to sunbathers and discourage fishermen during the day. Exercising your right to fish in public waters below the high-tide line (that is the law in most Northeast states) on state-run or privately maintained beaches where life guards are on duty is generally more hassle than it's worth, however. These beaches are far less crowded in the off-seasons of June and September when the fishing is perhaps best anyway.

Above all else, It is important to be constantly aware that the Northeasts' spectacular beaches are for everyone. Anglers must keep this in mind, regardless of where and when the fish show up. Prudent anglers who carefully work around bathers and beach-walkers are rarely bothered and instead they are often cheered by galleries of fascinated onlookers when they hook, play and release a trophy striper. When beaches become so crowded that fishing becomes frustrating it is a wise angler who elects to put the rod down and spend a day observing his quarry to better understand its behavior in preparation for another day.

An ideal sight-fishing beach has a wide, flat profile with fine sand and clear water that provide a consistently wadable intertidal zone flat.

Ocean Waves

Sight-fishing beaches are in direct contact with the open sea, which ensures clean, clear shoreline water and provides the endless influx of waves that are the pulse of the intertidal zone. Wave fields of all types influence ocean beaches. As with other factors that govern the quality of sight-fishing on any given day, the wave element presents a spectrum of impact ranging from ideal to unfishable that must be understood. Flat-calm days are splendid, but they are also rare. A meteorologically perfect day with light wind, blue skies and bright sun may prove disappointing with a pounding 10-foot surf making everything a froth of white-water from the water's edge to depths well over your head.

Ocean waves are generated by wind blowing across the sea's surface. Resulting wave height, wavelength (distance between wave crests) and the energy associated with wave field depends on the velocity of the driving wind that created it, the length of time it blew over the water, and the distance over which it blew. The resulting wave field controls the nature of the surf along a shoreline. While most wave conditions produce fishable surf, some do not. Some knowledge of physical oceanography will clarify why the nature of incoming wave fields along ocean beaches makes sight-fishing these shorelines so conditional.

Inshore flats are blessed with full geographic protection from waves. Offshore flats are surrounded by shoal-lines and islands that break ocean swells, protecting the interior flats as reef-lines do with tropical flats. Beachfronts, on the other hand, are vulnerable to waves of all types. Some wave fields, such as those resulting from daily afternoon onshore breezes, are created locally and are known as wind-chop. Others are the remnants of distant ocean storms and may persist for days or weeks. These deep ocean waves have long wavelengths capable of travelling hundreds and even thousands of miles at sea before making landfall along shores that had been otherwise entirely unaffected by the generating storm.

Ocean waves propagate over the surface of the water by a combination of wind and inertial forces. The energy contained

Overwhelming surf can shut down the sight-fishing very quickly.

A decaying swell makes landfall as well-formed waves arriving in sets.

in the wave field is transmitted along the ocean's surface so long as the water remains deep enough to prevent the subsurface fluid motion associated with each wave from contacting the bottom. The larger the wave, the deeper the water required for it to propagate. Small waves associated with wind-chop are erratic and dissipate quickly, usually within hours after the generating wind has died. Though wind-chop is chaotic, the waves are relatively small and most anglers easily handle the situation, often experiencing good fishing in these conditions.

Waves generated by offshore storms, on the other hand, are well-formed and contain a lot of entrained energy. The resulting wave fields are long-lived and often travel long distances at sea before making landfall, where they are experienced as swells. Ocean swells are large, well-defined waves that crest and break much further out than small waves do. The resulting surf can be overwhelming. The high surf associated with swells generally shuts down sight-fishing along beaches, sometimes for days, as the fish are no longer able to be spotted and the surf is simply too fierce for technical fly fishing of any kind. Very good fishing often results with a subsiding swell, however, as the surf-battered intertidal zone holds countless unearthed and incapacitated bottom forage creating an excellent feeding opportunity for stripers. Anglers can take advantage of this too.

Wave fields associated with ocean swells are not uniform. The swells propagate in packets, or "sets" as surfers refer to them. Most waves approach the shoreline in widely spaced sets during a subsiding swell. By focusing your efforts between these sets, when the surf has temporarily subsided, fish are readily spotted and well-timed presentations can be made to hungry fish.

With increased skill and experience, anglers may fish the surf with increasingly adverse wave conditions, but there is a point beyond which it is neither practical nor much fun. Of all the atmospheric and marine factors that influence the quality of surf-fishing conditions, adverse wave fields can shut down the fishing most quickly and absolutely.

Beach Profile and the Intertidal Zone

Sight-fishing beaches must have a gradual profile, or beach-face. A gradual transition from land to sea creates a shallow "flat" running parallel to the shoreline across which breaking waves roll in all but the most severe surf conditions. Steep beach-faces are indicative of a shoreline profile that drops off quickly and deeply at the water's edge.

As waves reach land their subsurface mechanics (orbital fluid motion) contact the bottom in shallow water. This contact slows waves down, causing the entire wave field to close ranks and ultimately they heighten, topple over and break. Consequently, shorelines that remain relatively deep right to the water's edge are incapable of slowing incoming wave fields, which inevitably crash right on the beach. The repeated hammering of waves on the beach-face results in a steep profile. These shorelines have strong littoral currents that transport churned-up sand, preventing the formation of sandbars and a shallow flat adjacent to the beach. The width of beach-face exposed between high and low tides (measured perpendicular to the shoreline) is also quite narrow making these beaches poor shorelines for sight-fishing.

Beaches with a gradual profile possess a significant band of shallow water adjacent to shore, known as the intertidal zone, across which incoming waves roll long distances as they dissipate shoreward. By intertidal zone (ITZ) I am referring (for angling purposes) to the band of shoreline that extends from the water's edge at high tide outward to the wave-break at low tide. The water movement here is complex, consisting of incoming waves, receding wash, tidal fluctuation, rip tides, littoral drift (water current parallel to the shoreline), and cross currents resulting from wind-driven waves. With moderate surf the principal water movement is the oscillating turbulent flow caused by waves rolling into shore and then receding back as wash.

Steep beach profiles cause waves to break on shore and they have a narrow intertidal zone, making them poor sight-fishing choices.

The ITZ is a fertile marine microcosm sustained by natural forces and it is the basis for a localized shoreline food chain of which the striper is king. Its importance to a beach's fertility and attractiveness as a gamefish feeding area are analogous to that of a tide marsh to an estuary. The ITZ is well nourished with decaying seaweed of all types. Eelgrass, kelp and other sea grasses are continually uprooted and wash ashore with onshore wind and incoming tides. They accumulate on the beach and in the ITZ where they gradually decompose (detritus) and become buried in the sand. Sea grasses are rich in nutrients and their decomposition while anchored in shoreline sands creates a nutrient-rich sediment base that supports many microorganisms, healthy bacteriological activity and the foundation for a strong and stable food chain.

ITZ biology is elegantly self-supporting. The very forces that enrich the shoreline with decaying organic matter, nourishing large numbers of organisms that consume oxygen and produce waste, also perpetually flush the ITZ of these toxins and replenish the oxygen through the action of tides and surf. Clams, sand fleas, crabs, worms and shrimp thrive here. Baitfish are drawn to the surf in large numbers for its rich food supply as well.

The wave action and turbulence in the ITZ surf creates an ideal feeding area for large game fish, especially striped bass. The bottom is constantly scoured by moving water, unearthing prey in the process. These prey are often injured or otherwise struggle to recover in the strong currents, which sweep them some distance along the bottom. Either way, the combination of weak, vulnerable prey and strong currents make the ITZ irresistible to large bass, which thrive here.

The clear water and relatively wide, flat contour of the ITZ make it ideal for stalking these fish. The complex currents, multiplicity of concurrent prey, and the wariness of the large stripers found here make it a challenging and exhilarating sight-fishing environment. To effectively sight-fish the surf, fly-fishers must become acquainted with ITZ water movements as well as striper feeding patterns and be able to anticipate each to some degree.

Shoreline Orientation and the Sun

Northeast beaches lie in many different orientations. To spot fish, anglers must have the sun at their backs for optimum viewing. The lay of the beach, be it east-west, north-south, or somewhere in between, has particular significance where sight-fishing is concerned. Shoreline orientation relative to the sun's track through the sky defines optimum directions for wading as well as the beach's overall sight-fishing quality.

East-west beaches are inherently the best for spotting fish. E-W beaches with northern ocean exposure are ideal as they allow a westerly wade in the morning, perfect seaward viewing with the sun at your back through midday, and an easterly wade in the afternoon. E-W beaches facing the sea to the south also provide good viewing throughout the day. However, the midday sun tracks through the Northern

Hemisphere sky slightly to the south creating minor glare in the angler's viewing window when looking seaward on these beaches.

North-south beaches have inherent sight-fishing limitations. The sun's east-to-west movement through the sky casts a formidable glare on the water in the morning for beaches facing the sea to the east, while beaches facing to the west experience high glare in the afternoon. In both cases, N-S beaches offer half-day fishing at best. This problem may be circumvented during low-tide periods with low surf when anglers can walk out a considerable distance from shore and wade parallel to the shoreline, looking shoreward for fish with the sun at their backs now.

Bottom Texture, Nutrients and Forage

Sight-fishing beaches must have light-colored, fine-sand bottoms. Cruising bass and the shadows they cast contrast well against a light bottom, which provides an ideal backdrop for spotting fish. Fine-sand bottoms support prey that burrow in them for cover and subsist on the rich nutrients they contain. Some beaches have loose granular bottoms that do not collect adequate organic matter and they are unsuitable burrowing media for most prey. Nearly every forage species that inhabits the surf relies on burying itself in the sand for survival. Beaches consisting of stones of any size are entirely unsuitable, as the movement of rocks in the surf would pulverize these bottom dwellers. Fine sand is ideal. Its nutrient base is continuously replenished with sedimentary microorganisms and decaying seaweed and its texture is perfect for burrowing prey.

Wind, Water Cleanliness and Temperature

In addition to its effect on wave generation, the wind plays an important role in water clarity and temperature along beaches. In general, water clarity remains high throughout the season along ocean beaches in contact with the open sea. Water temperature is moderated as well. However, during prolonged periods of onshore breeze (typical in the Northeast summer), shoreline water temperatures may rise above normal and clarity may diminish. Both effects are caused by the continual onshore push of warm surface water (heated by solar radiation) that is often slightly clouded with biologic activity. Such events are rarely significant enough to shut down fishing, but it is the relief brought by a period of counteracting *offshore breeze* that brings exciting results.

A shift to an offshore breeze initiates a flow of cool, clean bottom water into the surf, in the manner that upwelling occurs. Here, the push of warm surface water away from shore necessitates an inward flow of cool, clear bottom-water into the intertidal zone. Stripers react immediately to this and the action in the surf can be red hot as long as the wind blows offshore, which can last for days with slow-moving weather fronts.

Offshore breezes also improve sight-fishing conditions in other ways. The effect of wind blowing counter to the incoming waves can tame a wild surf in a short time, thus returning the surf to a sight-fishable condition. A prolonged offshore breeze can flatten shoreline surf to the point where only tiny waves remain that lap gently at the water's edge. Though infrequent, this surf condition greatly simplifies presentation, making the surf far easier to fish. When shoreline waters have become dirtied with excessive seaweed accumulation or clouded, due to a prolonged shoreline wave-break that churns the sand, an offshore breeze will clear the situation quickly by pushing water away from shore. Shoreline tidal movement subsequently carries these show-stoppers away.

Sand Structures

Beaches often appear as featureless coastlines. But in fact, when composed of fine sediment they are accented with unique sand structures that define the intertidal zone and influence the behavior of waves and shoreline currents. The land-sea interface is a system whereby the contour of the beach and its associated sand structures affects the behavior of the water, and the water, by way of wind-driven currents, waves and tides, in turn affects the shape of the beach.

Beach sand is in constant flux. The profile of the beach-face changes seasonally and the location, size and shape of sand deposits can shift from week to week (depending on waves and weather). These phenomena are complex to say the least and many physical oceanography texts are entirely devoted to the subject. For fishermen, however, knowing a few basic concepts can make this ever-changing environment a more understandable place to fish.

The general beach profile, flat or steep, changes seasonally along many shorelines in response to the buildup of sand on shore or in detached barrier sandbars running parallel to the water's edge. Along most shores, beach sand annually

RIP TIDE DYNAMICS

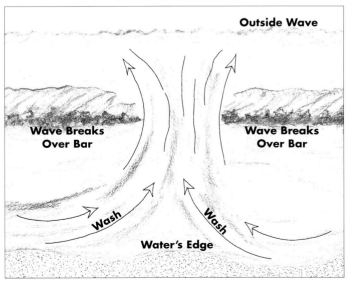

migrates outward in the winter, forming these sandbars, and returns again in spring under the action of prevailing onshore summer breezes to reform the flat beach-face. Severe storms at any time of the year can cause significant shoreline erosion, making a beach unrecognizable from its appearance prior to the storm. By similar forces that cause winter shifts, sands are gouged from the shore and deposited in outer bars or elsewhere on the beach downwind of the storm's onslaught. Shifting sand deposits disrupt existing concentrations of biomatter (referred to as "hot-zones" in Chapter Three) and create new ones. These shifts significantly affect the intertidal zone food chain and the foraging patterns of bottom-feeding game fish.

Two shoreline formations frequently occur that significantly influence the fishing—beach holes and sandbars. The two features are interrelated and generally one is not found without the other nearby. In fact, it is the presence of a sandbar formation that ultimately leads to the formation of holes under the action of wind-driven surf. Heavy surf, resulting from ocean swells, often rearranges beach sand to form outer bars. Wind-driven surf subsequently cuts through them at specific weak points to form holes in the surf. Holes are accompanied by rip tides that become increasingly powerful with increasing surf.

Sandbars form parallel to the shoreline from which they were created and typically run from 100 feet to several hundred yards in length. They act as a barrier to incoming waves and to the outflow of receding wash. The sudden shallow water causes incoming waves to heighten and break well out from shore and roll in as turbulent, well-oxygenated whitewater. Sandbars impede the receding wash, allowing suspended sand to settle and collect, thus further building up the bar. The environment here is in constant flux. What is important here for anglers is that along with sand, adult, juvenile and larvae of many prey are also scoured, shifted and deposited by the action of the surf in the vicinity of sandbars.

When onshore winds blow hard or for extended periods, the incoming surf becomes increasingly strong. Larger waves arrive on shore more quickly causing high volumes of water to move shoreward and buildup at higher than normal levels along the beach. Gravity, however, pulls this water back down to sea—powerfully. A sandbar can only resist the excess wash for so long before it gives way, allowing the built up head of water to spill out in a seaward flow. This outflow is not distributed evenly, however, but is concentrated at weak spots in the bar. Since massive amounts of water must recede through narrow openings through the sandbar, the flow is rapid and steady. Sand and prey are scoured as water rushes seaward, further weakening the bar at the breach point. This phenomenon creates a hole in the beach that we commonly associate with rip tides. The more powerful the incoming surf, the stronger the effects of the rip tide.

These two shoreline features are integrated beach phenomena—no sandbars exist for long without adjacent hole formations. Where and how many holes will develop within each bar depends on many complex surf and weather variables.

Large sandbars usually have many cuts through them, often at regular intervals. Small bars are usually flanked by a hole at each end. For sight-fishers, these are important features that concentrate prey and strongly influence striper feeding patterns. Sandbars collect and hold rich prey colonies buried in their sands, while rip tides funnel dislodged bottom-prey and baitfish through ideal game fish feeding lanes.

Currents and Tides

Tides and currents are less significant along ocean beaches, which are dominated by surf induced water movements. However, along every coastline there is a subtle prevailing current parallel to the shoreline known as littoral drift. This weak flow is often the result of prevailing winds in the area. Tides cause a gentle flow of water along a shoreline as well. Along most beaches the incoming and outgoing tides flow in opposite directions parallel to the shoreline; the strength of the tidal current increases as you move further away from shore. Depending on the direction of the tide, the flow works with or against the prevailing littoral current. When tide and littoral drift currents act together, the net result may produce a significant current. When they oppose one another, a negligible net flow results. Since stripers often feed with the current along beaches and relocate by moving against the flow, this can be valuable knowledge. In the absence of overwhelming wind-driven currents, the predominant direction of feeding stripers cruising *outside* the intertidal zone can be somewhat predicted by knowing the tide and the direction of the local littoral current.

Tides affect the nature of the surf, the behavior of the fish and how the beach is best fished in general. During the incoming tide, the water level along the beach rises and the fish often feed closer to shore. At high tide with low surf, stripers may be poking along right at the water's edge. At low tide they often concentrate further out on sandbars or outside the wave-break in calm water. When the fish are concentrating on large crabs found outside the wave-break, low tide is the only time they may be approached. Angling strategy must be adjusted to suit the tide and the resulting striper behavior.

Tides affect the quality of sight-fishing conditions to some extent as well. Incoming tides generally accentuate incoming waves, producing more aggressive surf. Sometimes this results in surf too strong, which degrades the fishing conditions. On the other hand, an outgoing tide reduces wave strength and surf, often producing better fishing conditions.

Water clarity is affected as well. Again, an incoming tide can rile up the surf, stirring up sand and clouding the water a bit. This effect is most pronounced at high tide. The outgoing tide suppresses the surf, pulls shoreline waters out and effectively clears the viewing. These tidal effects are subtle and one should not expect a simple tide change to miraculously subdue raging surf or clear up badly dirtied waters in a matter of hours. Tides merely fine-tune the surf conditions.

Chapter 2

Striped Bass Behavior in the Sight-Fishing Condition

Know Your Quarry

Striped bass behavior in the sight-fishing condition is unique. By "sight-fishing condition" I am referring to very clear, brightly lit shallow waters from one to five feet deep where the fish are readily spotted and presented with flies. A variety of surface activities visually reveal feeding stripers; the rise-forms left by fish sipping springtime worm-spawns and the wild splashing of bass blitzing migrating bait in the fall are examples. Casting to stripers under these conditions, however, is not what this book is about.

With clear, shallow water and bright sun, striper behavior is considerably different than what we're used to with night- or deep-feeding fish. Anglers should take time to carefully observe their quarry and learn its behavior. Since this fishing is entirely visual, there is ample opportunity to study the fish, its movements, and its feeding patterns. There is no substitute for being able to predict striper movements, to read which fish are feeders and which are not, and to somewhat read what the stripers are eating through their behavior.

Similarities to Bonefishing

Sight-fishing for striped bass and bonefishing have a lot in common. Both species are stalked in clear, shallow water where visual presentations are carefully made to moving targets that behave similarly. Both may be pursued on foot or by skiff, either alone or with a partner. It's no surprise that many bonefishers have enthusiastically taken to striper sight-fishing in recent years.

But the two sports are also very different, which experienced bonefishers must understand to consistently succeed with striped bass. Anatomical and environmental differences are most relevant and they influence many aspects of striper fishing. In my opinion, stripers pose a tougher flats challenge than most bonefish; the exception being the big bones found in the Florida Keys and northern Bahamas. Many comparisons to bonefish are made throughout this chapter to effectively highlight striped bass behavior and help those with bonefishing experience quickly adapt. Many books have been written about bonefishing, which are excellent background for striped bass sight-fishing.

Stripers Are at the Top of the Food Chain

Unlike bonefish, stripers have no natural enemies on the flats. The absence of barracuda and sharks on temperate northern flats allows stripers the freedom and comfort to graze the shallows without urgency. Bonefish, on the other hand, must have one eye open at all times for the jaws of death. With this in mind it's easy to see why bones are so skittish and often flush when spooked, while stripers appear calm and rarely become frantic when alerted to your presence. When alarmed, stripers often react by simply veering slightly from their course and merely maintain a safe distance.

Stripers encountered while sight-fishing typically run large. On inshore flats, fish from 25 to 32 inches long are common. Offshore flats and the surf offer even larger fish, with 30- to 44-inch fish typical. These stripers are from seven to 15 years old. They have been around a while, most likely have encountered many humans before, and are wizened and wary. Large stripers demonstrate what is known as a "sophisticated spook". This is best described as an acute awareness and respect for your presence, but without fear of harm. This is invariably accompanied by what has become a coined expression, "lockjaw", where the fish's mouth simply will not open for any fisherman's offering. The sophisticated spook takes some experience to recognize while it's happening. Large bass calmly continue about their business despite an angler's presence, and they seduce many rookie sight-fishers with their iron nerve. The only bonefish that maintain this calm on the flats are the large, osprey-proof variety, typical of the Florida Keys.

Stripers seem to get most agitated when they detect a skiff on the flats. Here, in addition to veering from their course they noticeably speed up to quickly get by the vessel. But they still remain calmer than bonefish. It takes some experience to interpret this behavior, which enables you to confidently ignore fish that have probably seen you and focus on those that have not. Many newcomers to this sport mistakenly conclude that stripers in this environment are "uncatchable" after they repeatedly fail to entice fish that had been alarmed by a non-stealthy approach.

Striper Feeding Behavior

Sight-fishing occurs in water temperatures of 60°F to 72°F; the warm upper range for striper activity. These temperatures occur in the summer when stripers have ceased migrating and have become resident throughout their northern range. The cool water temperatures associated with spring and fall trigger migratory behavior where striped bass become very active and feed aggressively on the baitfish that are also in transit. But during the summer the fish are much less active, eat less, and are quite casual about their feeding. The variety and abundance of forage available to stripers during the summer further adds to their selective nature, making them a challenging sight-fishing quarry. Summer stripers feed sparsely and

become noticeably leaner than voracious migrating bass. Most fish taken while sight-casting are thinner than average, according to accepted length-weight data for the species.

Striped bass possess large, reticulated stomachs, allowing them slowly fill their stomachs with large quantities of food and then not feed again for several tides (much like certain reptiles that feed and then don't eat for long periods). In contrast, bonefish have smooth, narrow stomachs that process food quickly, so they must feed often and at regular intervals. As a result, bonefish are more predictable than stripers. In addition, bass have many reliable ways of securing food; cruising the flats is just one option, while bonefish rely mainly on the flats.

Several factors, including the threat of predators, the need to feed regularly and the limited window for feeding controlled by the tides, combine to make bonefish opportunistic feeders. When they see something edible they usually go for it and devour it, especially when they first hit the flats at the top of the tide. As a result, fly selection is often not a challenge and seldom is there a need to survey the local prey as part of the selection process. Most bonefish destinations have a certain style to their flies, but many patterns will interest the fish much of the time. Some destinations certainly boast large, picky bones, but I think this is more a case of educated fish not being fooled by very many patterns anymore, giving a false impression of selectivity. I believe these educated fish will still eat a wide variety of naturals if the opportunity prevails.

Stripers are a different story alltogether. They cruise the flats without fear of predators and they do so by choice, not by necessity. There are other times and places for them to feed so they're in no rush. Furthermore, their time on the flats is not rushed by the ticking of the tide clock; they are quite casual and selectively feed on certain prey.

So what does all this mean to the angler? Are these fish impossible to dupe with a fly? Hardly! They do, however, require that you offer them what they're looking for, and present it well. Surveying the prevailing natural prey is very important when sight-fishing for striped bass and fly patterns are selected based on these observations. Selective stripers will often ignore all but one, occasionally two, imitations of the local prey. The long follows that stripers are notorious for when pursuing a fly reflect this selectivity; they scrutinize the fly before pouncing on it or turning off in a sudden refusal.

The way striped bass move across a flat is indicative of whether they are feeding, in transit to a different location, or in full-blown migration. Generally, slow-moving fish are feeders while fast-moving fish are in transit and tougher to interest with a fly. Unlike bonefish, which almost always feed into the tide, stripers feed both with and against the current. In fact, stripers often tip down and angle themselves 45° to the current and let the tide push them over the flat as they hunt. I consider fish in this feeding posture to be prime targets—they're slow moving and ready to feed. On offshore flats, meandering stripers are likely feeding and it is well worth the effort to pole into casting range. Schools of fish are frequently encountered on offshore flats. They are migratory, but still present a great opportunity as they often become competitive for food and several fish will see your fly simultaneously.

CHART C1

Striped Bass Length-Weight-Age Relationships (typical)

(inches - pounds - years)

Length	Migratory Weight	Summer Weight	Age
16	3	2.5	3
20	5	4	4
24	7	6	6
28	10	8	7
32	14	12	9
34	17	14	10
36	19	16	11
38	22	18	12
40	26	22	13
42	29	25	14
44	34	28	15
46	38	33	16
48	44	37	17

Singles, Pairs and the Resident School

On inshore flats and in the surf, the fish are usually encountered as singles or in pairs. Several fish working an area often arrive as a school, but quickly split up as they hunt. Throughout their stay on the flat, these fish periodically regroup in pairs or triples and then disperse again. This behavior is perhaps a strategy to graze more of the flat when the forage is spread out. To the angler this means that you must be careful not to spook *any* bass; alarming a few fish will eventually put all of the fish in an area on alert. They can communicate danger to one another by some means, which is why sloppy wading or the presence of a skiff on a small flat quickly shuts the fishing down.

Even though stripers are often spotted as singles, they are not entirely lone wolves. They are members of a nearby resident school. Resident schools may feed together after dark, but they spread out while on the flats and feed alone. It's important to note that not all members of a resident school will mount the flats in daylight. A certain percentage of them seem to be shallow-water specialists, and prefer this manner of feeding. This conclusion is based on my own tagging efforts that revealed the same bass working certain inshore flats and beaches over the course of a season. These areas invariably held more feeding fish after dark; most were much smaller than the fish spotted during the day. Perhaps age and size influence when stripers become ready to work the flats by day.

Stripers but alone, like this 30-pound cow...

— Striper Movements —

Offshore Flats

On offshore flats, stripers are typically found in schools, migrating northbound in the spring and southbound in the fall. Many schools hold over prey-rich flats and feed for several days before resuming their journey. In midsummer the schools thin out and fewer fish are found here in general. However,

...or in pairs, like this brace of 10-pounders.

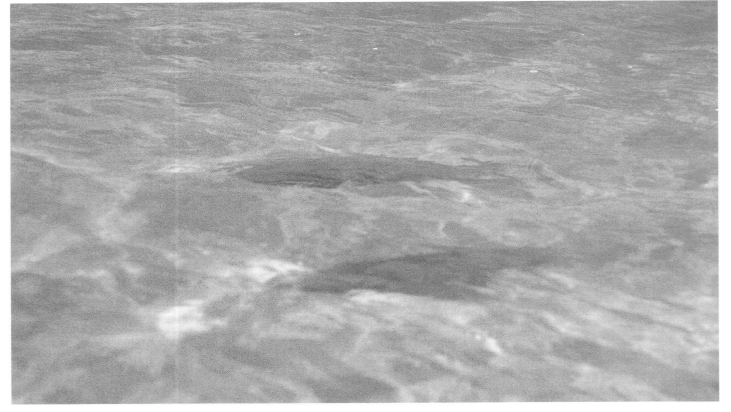

summertime schools are still far more prevalent offshore than on inshore flats or sight-fishing beaches, where they are seldom encountered.

Offshore schools are spectacular sights where impressive numbers of fish (routinely in the hundreds) move across the open flats in waves. Adjacent to islands, along grass shoals or running parallel to other structure, schools commonly stretch out lengthwise and parade along the structure in a seemingly endless progression of fish. School movements are largely influenced by tides where the fish prefer to migrate into the current.

Large numbers of fish do not necessarily mean that the fishing will be fast and easy. Many of these migrating fish are more interested in crossing the flat than chasing a tiny bit of food. Much like tarpon transiting tropical flats in spring, stripers (especially the large ones) migrating over offshore flats can be difficult to entice with a fly. Everything must be right to fool the big fish—fly, presentation and your stealth. The sheer numbers of fish in these schools make them great targets for presentation. Early-season fish, arriving in May and June, are often more aggressive than the stripers encountered later in the season. This is most likely the result of carryover migratory feeding in waters that are still relatively cool.

Single fish and small groups, or pods, are also found here. Again, fish moving quickly in one direction are likely in transit and unlikely to feed. Small groups of relocating fish often swim in strings (head-to-tail in single file). Strings of bass may look like tempting school configurations to cast to, but in fact they are very difficult as they are not feeding and are easily spooked. Slow-moving or meandering fish are good targets as they are most likely foraging on the bottom.

Inshore Flats

Most of the striper's non-feeding movement occurs in channels and in deep waters adjacent to inshore flats, while every fish spotted *on* the flats is likely feeding. They work the current-swept open flats both with and against the tide. Generally, fish feed into the tide quickly, staying on course in one direction. When feeding with the current, they do it slowly, and meander about in the process. They progress at about the same speed as the tide, which they use to push them along. Anglers should account for this in their presentation and not lead these slow-moving fish too far since the current naturally carries the fly away from them.

Stripers love to work edges. During high tide they take advantage of high water levels and slowly prowl the shoreline for crabs and small baitfish that use the banks for cover. They often cruise well into shoreline coves and tidal outflows as they feed. There may be a bass wherever the water is deep enough along the water's edge. At low tide, stripers cruise the edges of drop-offs where the water is still deep and schooling prey is often concentrated. They meander on and off the flat as they travel the edge. Strings of bass are commonly seen moving quickly into the tide along these same edges, but they are usually uninterested in chasing flies and are not good targets.

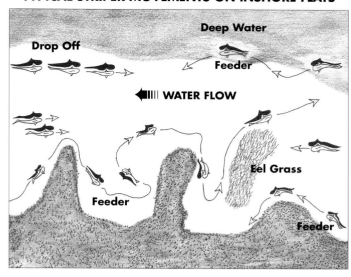

Stripers use channels within inshore flats for both travelling and feeding. When travelling they swim along the bottom of deep channels where the current is less and they usually remain unseen. Shallow channels, however, make great feeding lanes where shrimp and small baitfish are swept down tide in the current. They typically run one to three feet deeper than the surrounding water and with good light bass are easily spotted. Stripers may swim into the current as they pursue baitfish, or hold along the bottom and intercept fragile prey, such as shrimp and juvenile flounder, that drift with the tide.

When stripers work grassy shoreline edges at high tide, anglers should back 10 feet away from the edge to stalk them.

The Surf

In the complex surf environment, with intricate hole and sandbar formations, continuously changing currents and waves, striper movements are also complex. Striped bass work the surf both outside the waves, in parallel tracks along the beach and inside the waves throughout the intertidal zone.

Fish moving parallel to the shore are known as "cruisers". They may be very close to the water's edge on a high tide with low surf, or they may be well outside the wave-break at low tide. When cruising the shoreline, either in close or outside the waves, slow-movers are again feeding while fast-moving fish are not likely to break from their track to chase a fly.

Fish working the intertidal zone are known as "surfers". These fish are always solitary and they move in wave-like patterns as they feed. Surfers work the intertidal zone by meandering through it as they progress down the beach, or they may follow a parallel track spiked with sudden shoreward rushes behind rolling waves into the zone. Stripers surfing the intertidal zone are actively feeding and usually move fast in this agitated water—they are very good targets. Bass are commonly encountered gliding through the wash as the foam dissipates in a foot of water. These shallow-water surfers can appear suddenly out of nowhere, surprising even veteran sight-fishers, making this fishing extremely exciting.

Stripers probe every surf feature, investigating every possible opportunity for food, and they know them all. Sandbars, holes (rip tides) and sand plumes (muds), are three favorites. Sandbars form along shallow-profile beaches and they often hold prey. They are frequently flanked by holes, or rip tides that are cut in the bottom by the surf. Stripers search these sandbars for prey that is swept in the currents associated with the adjacent rip tides. They enter these holes from outside the surf, swim into shore and then return outside through the same hole and continue down the beach. Other times, when a sandbar is particularly fruitful, they comb the whole bar by entering through one hole, swim parallel to the sandbar and exit through a different hole at the other end. Stripers often repeat this pattern, thus circling the sandbar. Bars are on the

When the tide and waves are right, the surf produces a series of "muds" that stir up prey along the water's edge.

TYPICAL STRIPER MOVEMENTS IN THE SURF

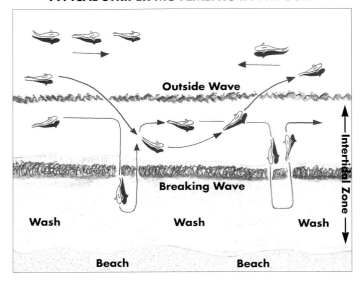

SOME FISH ENTER AND EXIT THROUGH THE SAME HOLE, OTHERS DO NOT.

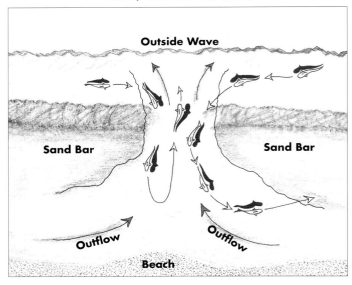

STRIPERS FOCUS ON SANDBAR HOT ZONES

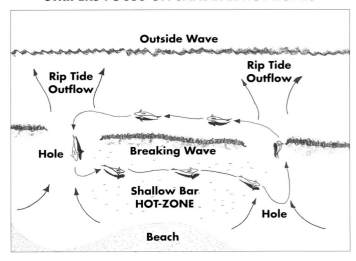

Sight-Fishing for Striped Bass

order of 100 feet or more in length and one time around the entire formation can take 10 to 20 minutes.

When the surf is breaking on the beach, as opposed to rolling in from further out, dense sand plumes or muds, are created very near shore with the crashing waves. These muds contain all sorts of unearthed surf-prey that gets pushed out in the plume and becomes easy prey for bass that dart in and out as they swim along the beach.

Striper Vision

The orientation of striper's eyes is typical of game fish designed for surface feeding, which the striper does so well. Bonefish, on the other hand, have heads and eyes oriented for bottom feeding and seeing predators off to the sides. They are less focused than striped bass on what's overhead. Stripers can pick up wading anglers, boats, fly lines and rod-flash at great distances. Their outstanding overhead vision influences the clothing worn for sight-fishing, the casting distances required, and many tackle modifications you will learn in Chapter Eight.

Fish see with a combination of monocular vision, for viewing to the side, and binocular vision for viewing things ahead and above. In addition to superb viewing of objects above, stripers have excellent binocular vision straight ahead that provides them an exceptional ability to perceive depth and movement. This allows them to focus sharply on objects ahead and gauge their speed very well. Stripers nearly always follow before striking a fly, and they rarely strike from the side. This behavior coupled with excellent binocular vision perhaps explains why the fly's action is so important to drawing strikes. The striper's tendency to suddenly lose interest during a follow when the cadence of the retrieve is varied (suddenly speeding up or slowing down the fly) most likely results from this as well.

Vertical Mobility

In contrast to most other flats game fish, striped bass feed throughout the water column. Bonefish, permit and redfish

Stripers have keen overhead vision that becomes quite binocular when looking straight ahead.

focus their feeding down toward the bottom, while tarpon primarily feed up toward the top. Bass are versatile and they may feed on the bottom, in the middle or near the top. Their feeding level relates to the prey species they're interested in and temperature gradients within the water column.

When feeding on crabs, flounder or other bottom forage, stripers remain focused on the bottom and rarely rise up for a fly presented overhead. When interested in sand eels, silversides or squid, which are found throughout the water column, they may readily respond to flies presented from the bottom to near the top (but rarely take surface offerings, such as poppers, in bright conditions). The depth that stripers are swimming is an indicator of whether they'll rise up or not. Fish cruising with their bellies on the bottom are not likely to rise for a fly while those at mid-depth will.

Water temperature and light levels also influence how high stripers are willing to feed. Bass are much more inclined to feed up during low-light periods, especially early morning sight-fishing. The surface water is also cool early in the day. Here, simple overhead presentations readily take fish. As surface waters warm with the rising sun, stripers become less and less likely to rise near the top and prefer to remain in cooler water near the bottom.

Vertical temperature gradients form within the water column when solar heating is significant. It appears that a temperature "ceiling" often results, which stripers are reluctant to cross. Tide changes and significant wind shifts (that mix warm surface waters) can disrupt thermal gradients and often result in afternoon flurries of striper activity. In the fall, water temperatures fall quickly with reduced solar warming each day and overnight radiant cooling on clear nights. Not surprisingly, stripers routinely feed top-to-bottom in the water column from September through the end of the sight-fishing season.

Color Changes

Stripers undergo changes in appearance to suit their surroundings and better camouflage themselves while on the flats. They adjust their appearance by altering skin pigmentation via biochemical processes that control the flow of certain chemicals through their blood. This process occurs automatically with most fish in response to the shade and texture of their surroundings. The range of color and shade is striking.

Stripers immersed in kelp beds or rocks become dark brown or green, while those that have been over sand become very pale and their stripes fade. The process is gradual and a fish coming onto the flats from deep, dark surroundings will become pale and well adjusted in about two hours. Stripers that remain on the flats for days turn almost white and the stripes nearly vanish. Dark fish on the flats are very good targets as they are recent arrivals and most likely hungrier and less selective than fish that have been on the flats for several hours or days.

Well-adapted stripers can be very difficult to see. Even 20- and 30-pound fish can become phantoms when they're fully adjusted to sand-bottom surroundings. Striper's sides also become quite silvery, reflecting the bottom around them, making them tough to spot at times; much like bonefish. In fact, there are times when the fish's shadow on the bottom is all that reveals its presence.

Chapter 3
Naturals

Knowing the food sources that draw striped bass to the shallows is vital to sight-fishing success for two reasons. First, your ability to recognize these prey helps in finding new sight-fishing waters and in assessing their quality as consistently productive flats. Second, unlike opportunistic bonefish, stripers are quite selective when grazing the flats under the sun. I'm not saying that bonefish are never picky, however they do come to the flats with a much more open mind than stripers do. Stripers rarely feed opportunistically and success depends on your ability to select fly patterns that reasonably imitate what the bass are focused on. In fact, reading the fish's feeding behavior, observing the forage and successfully matching the prey with your fly and presentation are a big part of this sport. Sight-fishing is much like trout fishing in this respect.

Regional Variation

Specific food sources found on different striper flats vary in response to several factors. On a regional scale, the abundance of each prey species varies throughout the Northeast. For example, large menhaden are more prevalent in the southern end of the striper's summer range, while herring and sand eels are most abundant in the northern reaches. Most prey relevant to this fishing is found throughout the Northeast to some degree, however.

The importance of each species at any point during the season will vary as you move up or down the coast. The relative abundance of these prey determines which become the primary food sources for stripers. On the Monomoy flats, for example, stripers may be focused on the large number of sand eels present in July, while southern New England fish have

long since lost interest in the few remaining schools and are now focused on large numbers of shrimp or crabs.

Habitat Preference

Knowing the habitat preferences of the prey is important when locating productive striper flats, as well as making fly selections while fishing unfamiliar waters. The prey inhabiting a given flat depends on the flat's environment and the type of habitat preferred by various species. For example, mole crabs thrive in the intertidal zone surf, but they are never found on offshore flats where no such zone exists. Other prey, such as green crabs, grass shrimp and mummichogs prefer the protected inshore flats associated with estuarine areas and are never found in tumultuous surf or on offshore flats.

Many forage species are migratory and are only temporary residents on certain flats that provide the right habitat during specific life cycle stages. Juvenile flounder and sand eels, for example, are important springtime estuarine prey that spend only their first few months of life there before moving seaward as summer nears. These temporary visitors are often present in large numbers, dominating the feeding picture until they move on.

Other species have flexible habitat preferences. Sand eels, silversides, and lady crabs are found in good numbers on all three flat types. Lady crabs, however, are particularly well adapted for survival in clear ocean waters and thrive along sandy ocean beaches and offshore flats. Migrating prey, such as sand eels, menhaden and silversides, are found on different flats during different stages of their migration. Sand eels again prefer protected estuaries in the spring, but later on as adults, they prefer the ocean waters associated with beaches and offshore flats during the summer. Mature silversides invade estuaries in spring to spawn, often well ahead of the sight-fishing season. As their offspring grow throughout the summer, they gradually exit inshore waters and become important on beaches and offshore flats later in the summer when they attain lengths greater than three inches.

Prey Distribution and Hot-Zones

The prevailing forage may be homogeneously distributed throughout an area, but more often it is not. Along beaches, crab populations are usually concentrated in colonies, or pockets, which create "hot-zones" along an otherwise uniform expanse of shoreline. Stripers are encountered more frequently and are more apt to feed in these areas. Much of this discontinuity results from beach and wave dynamics where sand deposits and subsequent sandbar formations collect larvae and other organic material, and form the foundations for localized prey concentrations. Marine worms

and baitfish populations also concentrate in these areas, further enhancing the richness of the hot-zone. You can bet the resident stripers along any beach know exactly where these zones are and where they have shifted to (beach profiles are constantly shifting due to wind and wave effects) throughout the season.

The formation of localized pockets of decaying seaweed (detritus), usually eelgrass, is another phenomenon that creates shoreline hot-zones. Marine vegetation grows rapidly in the summer and is routinely uprooted by storm and wave action and drifts ashore. Much of this weed collects along the tide-line where it dries and becomes buried with sand in the beach-face. During extended calm periods, this seaweed remains in the shallow water near shore and slowly decomposes. In time, this decaying matter blackens and coalesces to form distinct pockets of rich biomatter, which typically run 20 to 50 feet in length. The locations of these zones shift slightly along the beach, due to wind and wave effects, until they vanish. The nutrients concentrated in these areas attract crabs, shrimp, and baitfish, which feed

Prey variation in the surf—silversides, worms, mole crabs and sand shrimp—all found within 100 yards of each other.

within this micro-food chain. Stripers frequent these areas and also feed heavily in them. It may seem astonishing that something as subtle as a patch of decomposing sea grass can concentrate game fish along an otherwise featureless beach, but they do and I always look for them when fishing the surf.

Beaches also have significant habitat variation as you move perpendicularly away from shore. The prevalent prey varies from the water's edge through the surf zone to the calm water beyond the breaking waves. Worms, mole crabs and silversides are often found near shore in the agitated wash, while delicate sand eels and shrimp prefer the calm water and less disturbed bottom outside the wave-break. Lady crabs are a major food source for stripers along ocean beaches. They're very active swimmers that may be found among the rolling waves or beyond in deeper, calmer water. Generally the larger crabs prefer the less disturbed bottom outside the wave-break.

Inshore prey also prefer specific locations over the flat. Some estuarine species, such as green crabs and mummies, are permanent, non-migrating residents that concentrate near grassy or undercut banks from which they feed and find cover. During high water level conditions, when the tide is up and stripers have free reign over the shallows, silversides and sand eels also congregate in small schools near grass and deep-sided banks for the immediate cover they provide. Most estuaries are richly fed with nutrients from the adjacent marsh via tidal exchange from small cuts or channels running throughout the marshland. Baitfish must eat too, and this estuarine discharge provides a healthy nutrient supply for many prey, which concentrate outside channel and creek openings.

Sandbars are an integral part of the bottom structure of many inshore flats. Shrimp, various clams, and clam worms are normally concentrated on these bars, which collect larvae, transient sediments and other organic matter, thus creating fertile hot-zones. Sand eel schools, which burrow in fine sand for cover, are frequently found on sandbars.

Silversides, sand eels and juvenile flounder are also migratory and are found evenly distributed throughout the shallows as they grow and move out to sea. Stripers spread out evenly over the flats when grazing under these conditions. Posting–up or otherwise focusing your efforts on a specific zone is no longer a good strategy, but other opportunities prevail. The flats "open up" with this condition and wading over large areas becomes productive, allowing more anglers to sight-fish for longer periods throughout the tide.

Prey distribution over offshore flats is often controlled by the significant tides and currents typical of these big waters. Most forage on these flats (sand eels and herring in particular) are migratory, and tidal flow influences their location and movement. Features that concentrate prey movement include deep and shallow channels, shoal structure and islands. Eelgrass beds, clam beds and clam worm concentrations (frequently found in sandbars) are prey-rich hot-zones that attract feeding fish. Also, clam digging unearths all sorts of burrowing prey. Commercial clam diggers create man-made hot-zones both within the digging

area, as well as down tide, which always attracts hungry bass.

Offshore flats are generally associated with cool water. Areas within them that warm quickly, or to a higher temperature than neighboring water, often hold greater numbers of prey. The water on the windward side of islands and over dark grass beds heats up quickly, creating hot-zones in the process. Here, the wind moves warm surface water that builds up along windward shorelines. Dark bottoms effectively absorb solar radiation, which quickly warms the sediment, stimulating prey and biologic activity in the process.

Primary Prey Shifts and Selectivity

On the flats, stripers tend to focus on one food source at a time. Most times, only appropriately presented flies that imitate that prey will interest them. But many flats support *several* different food sources that draw the fish, however. Some food sources are present throughout the season while others appear and depart at different times as a result of their migratory schedule or life cycle progression. These facts present a challenge for the sight-fisher. The striper's inherent selectivity is perhaps the main reason why anglers who do not pay attention to these details find stripers frustratingly difficult on the flats. In general, stripers focus on the most prevalent food source (primary prey) on the flat at a given time. The length of time they remain on that forage may range from days to several weeks, depending on the relative abundance of other prey.

Prior knowledge of which food sources are indigenous to a flat, or will appear at each stage of the season, is invaluable. Fortunately, this information is fairly consistent from year to year for certain flats and primary food sources may be roughly patterned annually, much like a favorite trout stream. Serious sight-fishers are encouraged to keep logs of this information for the flats that they plan to fish often. An accurate, comprehensive Northeast flats-prey schedule is not possible, however. The impacts of large-scale seasonal weather variation (El Niño for example), commercial fishing and naturally occurring cycles within certain forage populations would make such a guide unreliable and often misleading.

Primary prey shifts are triggered mainly by the departure of the current food source or the arrival or proliferation of a new prey species. These two events do not necessarily occur simultaneously, but usually there is overlap as a new primary food source appears while an existing one is waning. Sometimes there is no overlap and the fertility of the flat or beach and its resident prey populations control how well the area continues to fish.

For example, when juvenile sand eels grow and depart an estuary, the stripers may exit with them if there are weak numbers of resident prey and an influx of a new primary food source, such as silversides, has not occurred yet. But when this sequence unfolds on fertile flats, stripers remain content by simply switching to a resident prey, such as crabs or shrimp, until the next significant migratory bait arrives or proliferates. Some flats do not sport versatile menus of spawning or migrating baitfish from year to year, but they have resident food in rich supply and continue to hold fish all season. Shrimp, crabs, killifish and worms are non-migratory inshore forage capable of sustaining striped bass throughout an entire season when found in large numbers. Worms, mole crabs and shrimp are resident coastline staples whose strong numbers can make ocean beaches resilient sight-fishing areas.

Most times, however, there is temporal overlap between primary prey species found in a given area. Stripers may be receptive to multiple offerings during two specific conditions. When transitioning between primary food sources they frequently show continued interest in the waning food supply and take flies that imitate both the old and the new primary prey for some time. This "grace period" is short however, and soon the new primary prey will be all that interests the fish; generally within a week or two.

Beaches and offshore flats offer a daily grace period for early morning sight-fishers. Here, stripers will continue to take flies that imitate what they were feeding on during the previous evening for some period into the day. Usually this is squid, a favorite nocturnal forage for striped bass. Once the sun is up, however, (about 10:00 a.m.) stripers again become fully focused on bottom forage and no longer rise for the transitional squid pattern. Spring worm hatches can also open the striper's mind somewhat while feeding on inshore flats in May and June. Carryover interest from a previous night's worm hatch often make bottom-working worm patterns effective on bass early in the day, much like the diurnal transition with squid.

Determining Primary Food Sources

Resident prey may be surveyed in a number of ways. Using polarized glasses, baitfish, such as silversides, sand eels and killies, are readily observed in the water. These small fish are

Sampling inshore bottoms with a net may reveal tiny crabs, shrimp, mummies and juvenile flounder, as this net did.

likely to be scattered in loose schools that are easily spotted near the banks of inshore flats in very shallow water. In the surf, silversides are easily observed in the shallow wash and as they nervously congregate around your feet to take cover. Offshore flats baitfish are generally larger (herring, mature sand eels, etc.) and they form bigger, more conspicuous schools that may appear as bait-clouds. They are easily observed at greater distances than the small, scattered baitfish schools associated with inshore waters.

Sea birds working the water are good indicators that baitfish are present. Terns, in particular, will give you excellent information. After diving on their prey, terns fly with their catch before eating it. If the baitfish appears stiff, like a twig, then it is a silverside. If it hangs limp, like a piece of cooked linguini, it is a sand eel. Baitfish may also be surveyed by setting a minnow trap. In a matter of hours, a trap baited with a piece of stale bread will hold every type of baitfish found in that area.

Crabs may be detected in a number of ways. The easiest is to simply look along the shore and in the water for them, which works best for green crabs. They often hide themselves too well and your best bet is to scan the banks and grassy shorelines for dried shells. When surveying beaches, scanning the tide-line for remnant shells is the only effective way to detect the presence of mole and lady crabs, which spend the majority of their time burrowed in the sand and out of sight.

Other flats prey, such as shrimp, worms and juvenile flounder, are not so easily detected. These are small, well-camouflaged creatures that frequently cover themselves with sand and are effectively revealed only by examining bottom sediments. A long-handled, fine-mesh net and a shovel are ideal tools for sampling bottom contents of a flat. I recommend that serious sight-fishers use them to profile frequently fished flats or whenever prospecting new areas.

Remnant lady crab shell along the tide line stripers are sure to be near.

Silversides
Menidia menidia

Silversides are small, schooling baitfish that range from two to six inches in length. They are found on inshore flats, off-shore flats and along many beach-es. In the surf they prefer depths of two feet or less in the intertidal zone wash where they remain on the bottom. On inshore flats they may congre-gate along marsh banks or other shoreline structure during high tide, but more often they are scattered throughout the flat. They are spawned in estuaries and juveniles appear on most flats about mid-July. They become numer-ous offshore and in the surf from late July through the end of August. Small up flies, such as chartreuse and white Blondes, sparsely tied olive and gray Deceivers and Johnny's Angel are excellent patterns on inshore flats where stripers often feed high on them. For bottom-feed-ing bass, especially along beaches, Clouser Minnows and Half & Halfs in various combinations of olive, gray, char-treuse and white are fine imitations.

Sand Eels
Ammodytes americanus

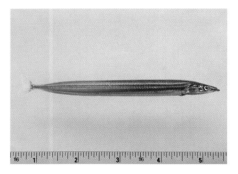

Sand eels are small, slim-bodied baitfish typically ranging from two to five inches in length. They are found inshore, off-shore and in the surf in small, tight schools that are often scattered throughout the flats. On the inshore flats of southern New England and Long Island, sand eels are most prevalent in the early season of May and June. The juveniles grow in estuar-ies and depart to outside waters in early July. In northern locations, such as Cape Cod, Martha's Vineyard and Nantucket, mature sand eels three to six inches in length are present in large numbers throughout the season. Sand eel schools are found throughout the water column, howev-er, they distinctly prefer the bottom and frequently burrow in fine sand to avoid predators or otherwise take cover. Small up flies, such as tan or yellow Blondes, sparsely tied brown and yellow Deceivers and Page's Sand Eel are all excellent imitations when they're swimming high. For bottom-

feeding bass, especially along beaches, Clouser Minnows in tan and yellow, or white with gold flash are fine imitations. Skok's Diving Sand Eel is an innovative pattern that mimics a burrowing sand eel and has proven to be quite effective on Martha's Vineyard. The Monomoy Special tied in olive or chartreuse is an effective imitation of the large sand eels found in the Chatham area.

Mummichogs and Killifish
Fundulus heteroclitus, Fundulus majalis

Mummies and kil-lies are small bot-tom-dwelling bait-fish that form loose schools that fre-quently spread out over the shallow bottoms of inshore flats. They typically range from two to four inches in length and they quickly take on the bottom coloration wher-ever they're found. Inshore flats, particularly those along estu-aries are ideal habitat. Mummies and killies prefer shoreline edges that provide excellent grass cover of undercut banks and marshes. These are non-migrating baitfish present on inshore flats throughout the season. The early season of May and June, however, is when they're most likely to be a primary food source for flats-feeding bass. Small deep-working flies such as olive or brown Clouser Minnows and Half & Halfs make excellent imitations.

Menhaden
Brevootia tyrannus

Menhaden (known regionally as bunker or pogies) are a significant Northeast food source for stripers, both on and off the flats, from August through October. These are large baitfish, rang-ing from three to 12 inches in length, that form tightly packed schools generally found near the surface. During good spawning years these prolific baitfish can completely dominate the striper's feeding activity to the point that they cease normal flats-feeding behavior. Sight-fishermen consider the presence of overwhelmingly large schools of menhaden a curse rather than a blessing. When present in smaller num-bers, however, bunker become very important while flats-fishing. In this scenario, stripers continue normal bottom-feeding patterns on the flats, but will consistently respond to large bunker imitations, which they take aggressively.

Menhaden are important to sight-fishermen along beaches and on offshore flats in the latter half of the sight-fishing season. Large up flies, such as Page's Big-Eye Baitfish and the Flats Deceiver are all excellent patterns. Easy over-head presentations are all that are needed to get the bass to come to these big, easy-to-see patterns.

Herring
Alosa pseudoharengus, A. aestivalis, A. harengus harengus

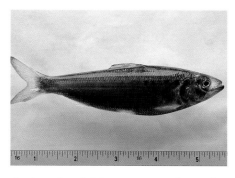

Herring are important prey for stripers wherever they are found. Throughout much of the Northeast, however, herring spend a good deal of their time on spawning runs in brackish and freshwater river systems during the fishing season. Along the northern reaches of the sight-fishing range they become significant food sources on ocean flats. Herring are large, schooling baitfish, which range from three to 10 inches in length. They form moderate to densely packed schools that are often quite large and easily spotted as dark, fast-moving bait-clouds. While on offshore flats, they feed within the nutrient-rich food chain, and thus schools may slow down, spread out, and become excellent prey for flats-feeding stripers. The ocean flats associated with Monomoy, Nantucket, and Cape Cod are areas where herring are significant prey during the sight-fishing season. Mark's Flatwing Herring, tied in shades of blue, is a pattern specifically developed to imitate herring. Other large up flies, such as blue and white Deceivers are also suitable patterns. These large, light flies are perfect for an overhead presentation. They are readily visible and effectively entice stripers from several feet away in a "non-hard-sell" fashion.

Flounder
Pseudopleuronectes americanus

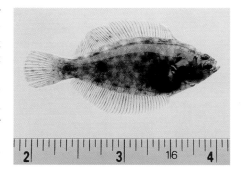

Juvenile flounder are prime forage for flats-feeding stripers throughout soft-bottomed, inshore estuarine areas that are used as nurseries for young flounder. Juveniles range from one to three inches in length, but do not school up. Instead, large numbers are found scattered over rich areas of the bottom. Flounder eggs hatch in these protected, nutrient-rich areas and the young grow quickly during the months of May and June. During this period they never leave the bottom as they move about the flats to feed. Certain areas of an estuary will hold more flounder than others; usually areas receiving marsh drainage, or run-off, are the most fertile and become hot-zones. During good spawning years, when flounder fry are numerous, stripers may focus on them for several weeks and ignore all other offerings. The juvenile flounder "hatch" subsides in early July when they are ready for outside waters and begin drifting seaward on outgoing tides. There have been very few fly patterns developed to imitate juvenile flounder. So far the most effective fly I have found is a Del's Merkin with the legs removed and the hook and eyes dulled with nail polish. The size, shape, coloration and action of this pattern are a perfect match. A strip-and-stop retrieve works well and the takes can be exciting as the angler watches the fish tip up on the fly, flare its gills and inhale it. A quick strip strike sets the hook.

— Crabs and Shrimp —

Lady Crabs
Ovalipes ocellatus

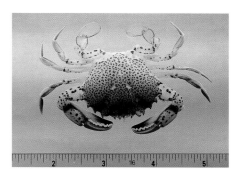

Lady crabs are perhaps the most important crab species for stripers and sight-fishermen. They are found both inshore and offshore and they are the main attraction for large bass working the surf. Lady crabs are fast and agile swimmers (as evidenced by their rear leg paddles) that feed aggressively on small fish and crustaceans, as well as scavenge the bottom. They prefer fine-sand bottoms into which they can burrow very quickly in order to ambush prey as well as avoid predators. The lady crab's eggs hatch in mid-summer, when waters are warm, and literally millions of tiny crabs may be found in nutrient-rich sediments. These tiny crabs, however, are not yet what the stripers are looking for. In most areas, the number of crabs one inch or more in diameter increases significantly by early August. Distinct concentrations of mature lady crabs may be found along beaches and in offshore areas, thus forming hot-zones. Crabs of this size attract large stripers that hunt them in daylight. Since they live in wide open sand flats, they survive predators by fleeing or burying themselves to take cover, both of which they do very quickly. They can swim quite fast. As such, traditional crab patterns intended to appear in a motion-less state do a poor job of fooling large bass. I have found that swimming crab patterns, such as the Pink Lady, which are retrievable are the most effective, especially in the surf. The Lady Calico Merkin, Simram and Chernobyl Crab are also good imitations that appear natural when retrieved.

Green Crabs
Carcinides maenas

Green crabs are important prey for stripers on inshore flats, especially those associated with estuarine areas. Green crabs favor habitat with some cover since they prefer to hide from predators rather than burrow. Inshore flats with eelgrass beds or solid marsh banks are sure to hold large colonies of green crabs. They are very important on inshore flats as they are non-migratory and found in good numbers throughout the season. Stripers frequently turn to the reliable green crab when other flats prey is in short supply. This occurs during primary prey shifts when the spawning or migration cycles of two primary prey species do not overlap, leading resident stripers to the shore banks for green crabs (which effectively makes greenies the interim primary prey). For this reason, inshore sight-fishermen should always have some green crab patterns on hand. Since they remain under cover during most of the day, stripers must nose about the bottom for them along undercut banks and marsh shores. Stripers also poke around in small weed patches in search of these crabs. Green crabs hide or remain still when stripers are near and dark crab patterns designed to remain stationary once presented are good imitations. The Green Crab Raghead, Puglisi Crab Fly, or a simple olive Woolly Bugger will all produce strikes. A good presentation allows the crab to settle on the bottom well ahead of the striper. Weak currents that carry the fly slowly enhance the presentation.

Mole Crabs
Emerita talpoida

Mole crabs, or sand fleas as they're sometimes referred to, are small, burrowing, claw-less crabs that inhabit the intertidal zone along beaches, often concentrated in localized colonies within nutrient-rich areas of the surf-bottom. They range from a half to two inches in length and, like marine worms, they remain buried; only exiting the bottom to relocate in or out from the shoreline as the water level rises and falls with the tide. Mole crabs are also unearthed (and often injured) by wave action and surf. They become available prey for stripers while relocating to new burrows as they tumble along the bottom with incoming or receding wash. The many egg-bearing females observed in June and July is evidence that mole crabs proliferate in the summer. These crabs are imitated by the Raghead pattern, which has little inherent action of its own and must be fished properly to draw strikes. The fly is cast into the wash ahead of an advancing striper. It is not retrieved, but instead is allowed to tumble in or out with advancing or receding surf. When timed properly the Raghead rolls in front of the striper's nose. The strike is very subtle and sometimes tough to read as the fish is advancing as it takes. Any slight acceleration forward toward the fly or quick flaring of the gills usually indicates a take. The Mole Crab fly developed by Terry Baird is perfect for stripers when tied in olive, tan or white.

Sand and Grass Shrimp
Cragnon vulgaris, Palaemonetes vulgaris

Small shrimp are important summer-time prey for stripers on many flats. In the Northeast there are two shrimp species important to stripers, sand (or bay) shrimp and grass shrimp. Both species range from one to three inches in length and they have a similar appearance. These shrimp are rarely found more than a few inches off the bottom, which they sometimes burrow in for cover. While sand shrimp are generally darker, both species are largely translucent and become virtually invisible when resting on the bottom. As their names imply, grass shrimp are often found throughout inshore grassy areas, while sand shrimp prefer the open sand shallows including the surf. Stripers show a pronounced interest in these shrimp in June and July, when their numbers swell from springtime proliferation. Stripers graze on shrimp on open flats and in beach surf, where bass slowly working the bottom along sandbars and outside the wave-break pick individual shrimp off the bottom and out of the sand. Here, small bottom-working down flies, such as a brown and white Clouser Minnow or a Crazy Charley work well with a slow, short-strip retrieve. On inshore flats, stripers often hold in shallow channels to intercept grass shrimp as they are carried with the tide. The fish rest on the bottom in ambush, but the shrimp drift several inches off the bottom. Here, flies that appear lifelike on a dead-drift work well. Lightweight up flies, such as the Simple One or Ted's Barn Island Shrimp, are perfect imitations when fished with a drag-free dead-drift presentation. Many times, a long leader (12 feet) and an offset upstream presentation, or a downstream presentation with a pile cast (which dumps excess slack in then water at the end of the cast) are the best ways to fish these flies in clear, shallow water.

— Other Flats Prey —

Squid
Loligo pealii

Squid are found along many ocean beaches and offshore flats in good numbers during spring and fall, however, they are present to some degree all season long. Squid remain deep for most of the day, becoming active throughout the water column at night where they feed on small baitfish. Opportunistic stripers feed on these squid at night, but often remain interested in them well past dawn into the sight-fishing day. Though not often seen on bright flats, squid feed in the shallows too—at night. They range from three to 10 inches in length and they are a primary food source for bass throughout the striper's range. Early morning sight-fishers achieve easy hook-ups while using squid patterns. Here, with relatively low light and cool surface water, stripers readily rise for a squid pattern presented with a simple over-head presentation. Lightweight patterns, such as the Magic Squid and the Half Hour Squid, are perfect for the flats. Without the heavy weighting common with many squid flies, these patterns land softly. They stay high and track level on the retrieve, which is important on shallow flats.

Clam Worms
Nereis virens, N. pelagica, N. limbata

Marine worms are important prey for stripers on the flats. Large clam worms, ranging from three to 10 inches long, are found in good numbers within most fertile bottoms where they mainly reside within the sand. The presence of worms is a strong indicator of an all-around healthy bottom and flats environment, much the same as with earthworms in a garden. They become food for stripers when they occasionally exit the soft bottom on their own, or when unearthed by storms or wave action in the surf. They are also uncovered in large numbers by clam diggers harvesting clam beds. By whatever means, large worms exposed along the bottom are rarely passed up by flats-feeding bass. They are particularly important to sight-fishers in the spring and early summer, when bass actively pursue various evening worm hatches. Their interest in worms carries over throughout the day during these periods and properly presented worm patterns easily take big fish. Long, undulating flies in pale colors, such as tan and pink work best. Heavily weighted patterns, such as the Zonker Strip Worm, remain on the bottom and draw strikes when used with a drop-and-twitch presentation.

CHART C2

Preferred Habitats and Seasons of Prey
(M-J = May-June, J-J = June-July, A-S = August-September)

Prey Species	Inshore M-J	J-J	A-S	Offshore M-J	J-J	A-S	Surf M-J	J-J	A-S
BAITFISH									
Silversides		●			●		●		
Sand Eels								●	
Mummies/Killies	●								
Menhaden				●					●
Herring									
Flounder	●								
CRABS/SHRIMP									
Lady Crabs		●			●		●		
Green Crabs	●								
Mole Crabs								●	
Sand Shrimp								●	
Grass Shrimp		●							
OTHER									
Squid	●			●			●		
Clam Worms							●		

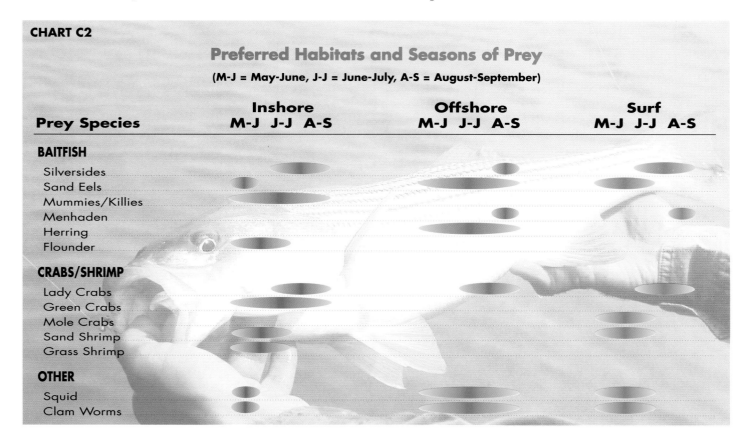

Chapter 4
Fly Patterns for Sight-Fishing

Effective fly patterns for sight-fishing may be classified in five basic categories: down flies, up flies, large flies, squid patterns, and crab patterns. Saltwater fly-fishers are familiar with many of these imitations, which are commonly used for stripers in general. Others are modified versions of familiar patterns, and some are unique to sight-fishing.

On the flats, striped bass may feed throughout the water column, but usually they're grazing on or near the bottom. They may move up to take a fly, but rarely do they take on the surface. The variety of prey important to flats-feeding stripers (from bottom-dwelling crabs to surface-schooling baitfish) is the reason why there are *five* broad classes of flies relevant to this sight-fishing, while for one-dimensional feeders, such as bonefish or tarpon, there are not. Some striper prey, such as silversides and sand eels, may be found naturally throughout the water column, and a variety of pattern types will work. Crabs, on the other hand, are bottom-dwellers and pattern choices are limited to weighted crab flies. Flies should be selected that work at or above the fish's cruising level since bass are designed for overhead feeding. Flies that sink below the level of a cruising bass will not be noticed and will not draw strikes.

I am not a believer in exact imitation. I believe that the power of suggestion coupled with the smooth salesmanship we call presentation creates hookups. Patterns that strongly suggest what the bass are grazing on through correct size, shape, color, depth, and *action* will draw strikes when presented properly. Striped bass scrutinize the action of a fly, and they rarely take a fly that is not moving (as bonefish and permit often do). I always consider a fly's action in my pattern selections. The hopping action of the Clouser Minnow is often very effective, but flies designed with hackle feathers, marabou or other action-oriented materials usually produce more strikes. Remember that most flats have mild water movement (in the surf this is true only outside the intertidal zone) in comparison to other striper waters, and the fish can closely examine an offering before taking. The most effective flies, including crab patterns, should therefore have some inherent action and not appear stiff in the water.

Considerations for selecting patterns are pretty much the same here as with other saltwater angling, with an emphasis on matching the hatch. Remember that stripers feed casually and are very selective on the flats. There is no substitute for experience in knowing what the bass are eating on a given flat at any given time. In fact, many sight-fishing guides know this so well that they have specific flies ready for each flat they fish throughout the season.

Every flat is unique and comprehensive coast-wide prey schedules are impossible to formulate with certainty. Forces of nature can alter the biologic activity in a region making such an encyclopedia of predictive marine biology a farce. While some degree of annual consistency prevails for various prey species in different regions, anglers will do better by determining what the bass are eating through on-the-water observation before selecting a pattern.

In general, bass on inshore and offshore flats feed consistently for several weeks at a time. Changes in eating habits are usually triggered by the departure of an existing, or the influx of a new primary food source. I caution you about making quick determinations here, this can be tricky. For example, there may be large schools of sand eels on a flat, but the bass' preference for the less conspicuous juvenile flounder may persist for days or weeks. During periods of primary food source transition, however, stripers tend to loosen up and take more than one imitation.

Fly selection is challenging when fishing the surf. The fish not only vary their diet throughout the season, they also vary it throughout daily tide cycles. As water level and wave action shift within the intertidal zone, stripers adjust their feeding in or out from the beach to take advantage of different opportunities. For example, the fish may shift from chasing silversides in the knee-deep intertidal zone to hunting lady crabs further out in chest-deep water as water levels drop with a falling tide.

Down Flies

These patterns are used when casting to bottom-feeding stripers. Since stripers on the flats are usually feeding down, these flies are used most often. They mimic the shrimp, worms, juvenile flounder, silversides, and sand eels commonly found on the flats. Just as the name infers, these patterns are designed to go to the bottom and stay there during the retrieve. Included in this class of flies are two of the most heralded patterns in saltwater fly fishing, the Clouser Minnow and the Crazy Charlie.

The hooks should be on the small side for better concealment, as with most flies for sight-fishing. You may miss a hook-up now and then, and occasionally have a hook straightened, but in the long run you'll hook more fish. Since these patterns are intended to be fished on the bottom, all of them are tied with up-riding hooks. Bottom-dwelling forage is never shiny or mirror-like (as with upper water column baitfish) and bright, up-riding hooks appear unnatural to the fish. Even silversides appear dull when viewed from above. Skeptical bass may follow a fly intensely but not eat it. When I encounter these fish I add some bland-colored nail polish to the bend and barb of the hook to suppress the shine. In fact, most of my down flies are tied on hooks with a dull finish, such as Tiemco or Eagle Claw, or the hook is treated with nail polish before the fly sees action.

One of the most effective flies for sight-fishing is the Clouser Minnow. The hopping action of this fly is deadly when imitating shrimp in calm-water flats. But it poorly represents a silverside in shallow water, which tracks evenly as it swims, rarely hopping in this fashion. Silversides are very important to stripers on many flats so I've modified the Clouser pattern to be more effective in fooling bottom-feeding bass that scrutinize the fly's action before striking. Weighting it less with lead eyes and more with lead wire on the hook shank, and adding two or four hackle feathers to the tail in the style of a Half and Half works wonders. These modifications allow the fly to track flat along the bottom and it now has vivid action in its tail, which will be right in the nose of a following striper who's looking closely at its movement.

Excited bass usually pursue the fly for a bit before striking from behind. Their vision becomes binocular when looking dead ahead, as opposed to monocular vision to the sides, giving them excellent perception of movement. I'm convinced that these two facts combined are the reason that actionless flies often fail to draw strikes when sight-fishing.

Another effective down-fly modification is the legless Merkin (a crab fly developed by permit specialist Del Brown). This fly becomes a superb juvenile flounder imitation in size, color and action when the white rubber-band legs are removed. If not already dull-finished, applying brown or tan nail polish to the hook and lead eyes is also recommended to suppress their shine.

Up Flies

When stripers are feeding up in the water column on high-riding bait, such as silversides, sand eels or drifting shrimp, the most effective patterns are up flies. These flies may be effectively fished at mid-depth with intermediate fly lines in water from one to four feet deep. In deeper water, often encountered on offshore flats, a full-sinking line is recommended to get the fly down a couple of feet.

Oh well, this happens from time to time, even with large hooks. The sudden, wild head-shaking after the hook-up is part of the sight-fishing excitement.

Up flies are designed to work high in the water column.

These important patterns imitate the shrimp, silver-sides, and sand eels, which are prevalent on every flat type. Two well-known patterns in this group are Joe Brook's Blonde and Lefty's Deceiver. One of the big advantages when fishing up flies is that simple overhead presentation is effective in water more than two feet deep. The overhead presentation is easy and it spooks few fish (see more in Chapter Six).

Deceivers have inherently good action in their tails when the hackles are tied splayed, in the manner of a Keys-style tarpon fly. Blondes pulse nicely and ride high and level during the retrieve when the bucktail is flared slightly. Johnny's Angel is a very effective, easy-to-cast fly that draws strikes through its unique reflection of light. The hooks should again be on the small side for concealment; sizes one through six are typical. Light-wire hooks are effective for high-riding flies, especially in very shallow water or when dead drifting.

Large Flies

At certain times of the season, particularly offshore and in the surf, large baitfish become the primary forage that draw the bass. Large bait is present to some extent on offshore flats all the time where very large sand eels, four to six inches in length, and herring are common throughout the sight-fishing season. Large baitfish appear along shoreline surf in the late summer and early fall. Migrating menhaden, and sometimes herring, make up the menu. When significant amounts of these large forage fish are present they can dominate the striper's diet and all other tidbits are ignored. Large flies make up the fly box for most offshore sight-fishing where the bass and the bait both run large.

Large flies may be fished throughout the water column. The right depth corresponds to the prevailing bait: sand eels from mid-depth to the bottom, and herring and menhaden from mid-depth to near the surface. I recommend that large up flies be fished with a full-sinking line rather than an intermediate. The water resistance (drag) of these flies causes

them to rise rapidly in the water while being retrieved. Flies that ride too high in the water provide a following fish a very good view of the angler, especially when fishing from a skiff. Fast-sinking fly lines minimize this and lead to more strikes. Some well known large flies are Lefty's Deceiver and Page's Big-Eye Baitfish as up flies, and the Half and Half, tied long, for working the bottom.

Squid Patterns

Squid are one of the striper's favorite, and perhaps most important, food sources throughout the season. They are most active during the evening hours, which is mainly when stripers feed on them. So one might ask why squid flies would ever be considered important for sight-fishing, which is practiced during the day. As described in Chapter Three, selective stripers often shift their primary forage, but sometimes remain interested in a prior food source for hours or even days after the shift. This phenomenon is displayed most clearly during the sunrise diurnal transition. Stripers that have been actively feeding on squid at night will continue to respond favorably to squid patterns and readily take them well after the sun has risen. Squid are common along ocean beaches and on offshore flats, but are found less often on inshore flats.

Stripers spotted early in the sight-fishing day can be easily enticed with a squid pattern. Carryover feeding on squid generally occurs from sunrise to as late as 10 a.m., but it takes careful spotting to see the fish this early in the day. On the other hand, the low light makes fly lines, leaders and anglers much less visible to the fish, which often rise in the water column to take flies presented overhead. These factors combine to make presentation and maintaining your stealth far simpler. Many fish are hooked in this fashion. With warm surface water and bright sun after 10 a.m., stripers become reluctant to rise and take high in the water column.

When they're willing to rise up to feed, however, the forgiving overhead presentation is effective, as fly place-

Large flies imitate the large prey found on offshore flats and in the surf.

The Magic Squid.

ment and the direction of retrieve are much less critical. Lightweight squid patterns with lots of action work best when sight-fishing. They far out-perform heavily weighted squid flies commonly used for deep-water fishing. The Magic Squid pattern was expressly developed for sight-fishing and it has accounted for over 300 hook-ups for me. It is lightweight, rides high in the water and has the right action for the slow-flowing waters associated with most flats.

Crab Patterns

Crabs are extremely important food sources wherever stripers feed on the flats. Lady, or calico, crabs are significant on offshore flats and in the surf, green crabs are predominant on inshore flats, while mole crabs are found exclusively in the surf's intertidal zone. In general, large fish prefer large baitfish and crustaceans over the smaller tidbits associated with the flats. As a result, many of the large bass encountered in shallow water are feeding on crabs, particularly in the surf. The crabs these large fish are most interested in, however, are relatively small; usually one to two inches in diameter. This is probably because small crabs are far more plentiful than large ones. Small crabs are readily imitated with a number of patterns, but for stripers, effective flies must have certain attributes.

Many anglers are not familiar with fishing crab patterns and much of what they do understand pertains more to permit than to striped bass. Stripers will, on occasion, take a stationary, permit-style crab fly, but more often they will not. Crab flies that are retrievable are much more effective on stripers for two reasons. First, lady crabs are burrowers by design. Unlike many tropical crabs, they live in sandy bottoms in which they can quickly bury themselves. Permit like to feed over coral and other hard bottoms that crabs cannot burrow into. These crabs resort to remaining still to avoid detection. Nearly all permit flies are designed to appear like a motionless crab, a sculpture of sorts. Lady crabs do not behave this way and crab patterns so presented are often

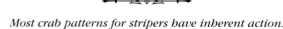

Most crab patterns for stripers have inherent action.

ignored and sometimes spook the large fish. A fly with crab-like swimming action that is retrievable is much more effective.

Secondly, stripers perceive motion very well when feeding on the bottom. In fact, they rely on it. A fly that resembles a fleeing crab, frantic to find a place to burrow, or perhaps injured in the surf and unable to bury itself (many small creatures perish in violent surf) gets more attention and dupes more stripers than stationary patterns.

Green crabs flee for cover as well; an undercut bank, a nearby patch of seaweed, etc. They too can burrow in soft bottoms and they are unlikely to sit still in the open and be gobbled up. Green crabs move more slowly than lady crabs and a fly that crawls along the bottom or that is swept with the tide is ideal.

Mole crabs are nearly always buried in the surf's intertidal zone soft-sand bottom. Their rapid burrowing makes them hard targets for stripers to hit, but when unearthed during changing tides, mole crabs move in or out with the advancing or receding tide. They are vulnerable at this time, as they roll along the bottom momentarily before quickly reburying themselves. Here again is a crab that, by its very nature, is in motion when stripers come to feed. The surf is a dynamic environment and it takes a fair amount of angler skill and experience to properly fish a mole crab pattern. The basic approach is to cast the fly into the wash ahead of an advancing fish and let it tumble along the bottom, just like the natural. If timed correctly, a well-placed mole crab fly will roll in front of the striper, which will inhale it quickly in a sharp, but non-violent take.

Crab patterns for stripers are unusual. The Pink Lady pattern was developed for imitating lady crabs in the surf. Its action mimics a lady crab darting along the bottom and it is heavily weighted to get it down quickly. The Mole Crab pattern, also intended for the surf, is heavily weighted as well. It has little inherent action, and the flow of the surf must be used to bring it to life with a well-timed presentation.

The Lady Calico Merkin, Green Crab Raghead, Del's Merkin, and the Puglisi Crab are all excellent crab patterns for striped bass. These flies are retrievable and work best in the calm waters associated with inshore and offshore flats where they require relatively less weighting to get to the bottom and appear natural. Enrico's fly is a fine green crab imitation, while Del's Merkin imitates both green and lady crabs. Remember, crab patterns may be easily modified to match surrounding bottom coloration (as the naturals do so well) with color marking pens. The unnatural shine of hooks and lead eyes may alarm some stripers but this can be quickly eliminated with nail polish (this can be done at home or while on the flats with a quick-drying product). In fact, I recommend hooks with dull finishes for all crab imitations.

One note regarding tackle when fishing crab flies; because these flies are heavy and wind-resistant, heavier tackle is recommended to get casts off quickly and accurately. The fish you'll most likely be casting these patterns to will also be large, and the heavier tackle is a nice fit there as well. Nine- and 10-weight tackle is ideal.

Down Flies

Del's Merkin, modified
(Del Brown/Umpqua Feather Merchants)

Hook: Mustad 34007/3407; Tiemco 811S; size 1/0-1
Thread: Danville's flat waxed nylon, chartreuse
Tail: Pearl Flashabou (optional); badger hackle
Body: Antron yarn, brown, tan
Legs: None or removed
Eyes: Nickel-plated lead, painted brown, tan or purple

Half & Half, olive and gray
(Alan Caolo)

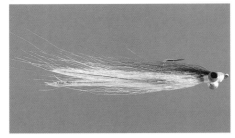

Hook: Mustad 34007/3407; Tiemco 811S; size 1-4
Thread: White
Tail: Blue dun hackle; pearl Flashabou
Body: Lead wire; pearl poly braid
Wing: Bucktail, gray, olive; pearl Flashabou
Underwing: Bucktail, gray
Eyes: Lead eyes painted black on tan

Clouser Minnow, brown and white
(Bob Clouser)

Hook: Mustad 34007/3407; Tiemco 811S; size 1-4
Thread: White
Wing: Bucktail, white, brown; silver, gold Krystal Flash
Underwing: White bucktail
Eyes: Lead eyes painted black on tan
Variations: Yellow bucktail in lieu of white; pearl Krystal Flash in lieu of gold

Clouser Minnow, white and gold
(Bob Clouser)

Hook: Mustad 34007/3407; Tiemco 811S; size 4-6
Thread: White
Wing: White bucktail; gold Krystal Flash
Underwing: White bucktail
Eyes: Lead eyes painted black on tan or red

Clouser Minnow, tan and gold
(Bob Clouser)

Hook: Mustad 34007/3407; Tiemco 811S; size 1-4
Thread: White
Wing: Tan bucktail; gold Krystal Flash
Underwing: Tan bucktail
Eyes: Lead eyes painted black on tan

Zonker Strip Worm
(Alan Caolo)

Hook: Mustad 34007/3407; Tiemco 811S; size 2-6
Thread: Pink
Tail: Tan rabbit strip
Body: Lead wire; tan rabbit strip, cross-cut
Eyes: Lead eyes painted tan
Modification: Mark red line along Zonker strip back

Crazy Charlie
(Bob Nauheim)

Hook: Mustad 34007/3407; Tiemco 811S; size 2-6
Thread: White
Tail: Pearl Krystal Flash
Body: Pearl Flashabou; mono
Wing: Creme hackle
Eyes: Silver bead chain

Skok's Diving Sand Eel
(Dave Skok)

Hook: Eagle Claw 254SS; size 1
Thread: Clear mono, fine
Tail: Ostrich, white, ginger; gold Sparkleflash
Body: Pearl E-Z Body tubing, small
Outriggers: 12# Mason; tied perpendicular
Eyes: Brass, small or x-small
Modification: Mark body tan with olive bands, black lateral line

Jiggy
(Bob Popovics)

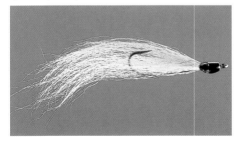

Hook: Tiemco 911S, bendback optional; size 1-4
Thread: Fine monofilament
Wing: Bucktail, white, tan
Head: Jiggy head, silver or gold; Devcon clear five-minute epoxy
Eyes: Self-sticking prism eyes
Modifications: Wing material; Ultra Hair, Super Hair, rabbit fur, chartreuse, olive; Krystal Flash, pearl, silver

Lefty's Deceiver, olive and gray
(Lefty Kreh)

Hook: Mustad 34007/3407; Tiemco 811S; size 1-4
Thread: White
Tail: Hackle, blue dun, olive; pearl Krystal Flash
Body: Pearl poly braid
Wing: Bucktail, gray, olive
Eyes: Black paint
Modification: Tied sparse, no collar

Irish Blonde
(Joe Brooks)

Hook: Mustad 34007/3407; Gamakatsu SP11-3L3H; size 1-4
Thread: White
Tail: White bucktail, pearl Krystal Flash
Body: Pearl poly braid
Wing: Chartreuse bucktail
Eyes: Black paint

Argentine Blonde
(Joe Brooks)

Hook: Mustad 34007/3407; Gamakatsu SP11-3L3H; size 1-4
Thread: White
Tail: White bucktail, pearl Krystal Flash
Body: Silver poly braid
Wing: Light blue bucktail
Eyes: Black paint

Page's Sand Eel
(Page Rogers/Umpqua Feather Merchants)

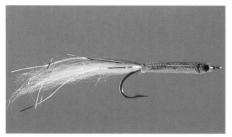

Hook: Mustad 34011; Eagle Claw 066SS
Thread: Danville's flat waxed nylon, white
Tail: Fly Fur, white, chartreuse, green; Flashabou, silver, lime-pearl
Body: Pearl Mylar tubing; epoxy
Gills: Painted gloss red
Eyes: Witchcraft 2EY, black on silver
Modification: Body marker-colored light green on sides, dark green on top

Simple One
(C. Boyd Pfeiffer)

Hook: Eagle Claw 254SS; Mustad 34007/3407; Tiemco 811S; size 2-6
Thread: White
Body: Silver poly braid
Collar: White bucktail
Modification: Pearl Krystal Flash in collar

Johnny's Angel
(Johnny Glenn/Orvis Co.)

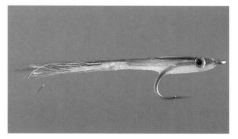

Hook: Eagle Claw 254SS; size 1
Thread: Danville's flat waxed nylon, white
Wing: White Superhair; Multilight Glimmer; olive FisHair
Lateral Line: Pearl Mylar strip
Eyes: Prismatic eye; size 2
Coating: GE Household Silicone; two coats

Ted's Barn Island Shrimp
(Ted Hendrickson)

Hook: Mustad 34011; size 4-6
Thread: White
Body: Wood duck dyed mallard breast
Antennae: Pearl Krystal Flash; tan bucktail
Swimmerets: Pearl Estaz
Legs: Pearl braided mylar tubing, 1/8"
Lower Head: Pearl braided mylar tubing, 1/8"
Upper Head: Olive hackle tip
Eyes: Melted mono, 40#-50#, epoxy

Surf Candy
(Bob Popovics)

Hook: Tiemco 800S; size 1-4
Thread: Fine monofilament
Body: Silver Mylar tinsel
Wing: Ultra Hair, chartreuse, gray; rainbow Flashabou, Devcon clear five-minute epoxy
Gills: Red Sharpie permanent marker
Eyes: Self-sticking prism eyes
Modifications: Wing material; Super Hair, Craft Fur, chartreuse, tan; pearl Krystal Flash

Ultra Shrimp
(Bob Popovics)

Hook: TMC 811S; size 1/0 and 4
Thread: Tan 3/0
Tail: Tan Ultra hair; gold Krystal Flash
Body: Tan Ultra Hair, cut to shape and epoxied, over tan thread palmered with brown hackle
Antennae: Tan Ultra Hair
Eyes: Burned monofilament, colored black

Large Flies

Monomoy Special, blue
(Kris Jop)

Hook: Mustad 34007/3407; size 2/0-1
Thread: White
Tail: Hackle (long), blue grizzly, white; Flashabou, pearl, silver
Wing: Blue bucktail or Fish Hair
Underwing: White bucktail
Eyes: Witchcraft 2EY, black on silver
Variations: Tail: olive or chartreuse grizzly; **Wing:** Olive or chartreuse

Rogers' Big-Eye Baitfish
(Page Rogers/Umpqua Feather Merchants)

Hook: Tiemco 800S; size 2/0
Thread: Danville's flat waxed nylon, white
Body: White hackle; Fire Fly Tie, pearl, silver
Throat: White bucktail; red wool
Shoulder: Gray bucktail
Topping: Pearlescent Fly Flash, olive, black; peacock herl
Eyeplate: Silver prismatic tape
Eyes: Witchcraft adhesive; black on orange
Variations: Bunker (blue and white)

Flats Deceiver
(Lefty Kreh)

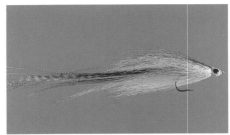

Hook: Mustad 34007/3407; size 2/0-1/0
Thread: White
Tail: Hackle (long), ginger grizzly, olive; pearl Flashabou; gold Krystal Flash
Body: Lead wire; gold poly braid
Top collar: Bucktail, tan, olive
Mid-collar: Pink bucktail
Bottom collar: Bucktail, tan, gray
Eyes: Black paint
Variations: Tail, light blue, white; collar, blue, pink, white

Tide Rip, chartreuse
(Tom Kintz)

Hook: Tiemco 811S; size 4/0
Thread: Clear mono
Body: Pearl poly braid
Wing: Saddle hackle, white, chartreuse
Underwing: White bucktail; Flashabou, pearl, chartreuse
Topping: Pearl Flashabou
Eyes: Crystal Eyes, large with epoxy pupil
Variations: Wing: olive

Half & Half, olive and gray
(Alan Caolo)

Hook: Mustad 34007/3407; Tiemco 811S; size 1/0
Thread: White
Tail: Gray bucktail; gray hackle (long)
Body: Lead wire; pearl poly braid
Wing: Olive bucktail; olive hackle (long); pearl Flashabou
Eyes: Lead eyes, large; painted black over tan or white
Variations: Creme tail; tan wing; gold Krystal Flash

Mark's Flat Wing Herring
(Mark Lewchik)

Hook: Mustad 77660 SS or Tiemco 800S; size 4/0-2/0
Thread: Danville's flat waxed nylon, white
Tail: White bucktail; saddle hackle, white, pink, yellow; Flashabou, pearl, pink pearl, silver, gold, blue pearl
Wing: Bucktail, white, pink, yellow, light blue; Flashabou, pink pearl, silver, gold, blue pearl; blue saddle hackle tied flat on top
Body: Bill's Body Braid, silver
Eyes: Molded eyes, silver or gold

Squid Patterns

Magic Squid, pink
(Alan Caolo)

Hook: Mustad 34011; 1/0
Thread: White
Tail: Hackle, blue, pink, white; pearl Flashabou
Body: Pink rooster tail (very wide), palmered
Eyes: Bead chain, large, painted black

Watch Hill Squid
(Tom Kintz)

Hook: Tiemco 911S; size 2-4/0
Thread: Clear mono
Tail: White hackle; pearl Krystal Flash
Body: Pearl poly braid
Rear Collar: White calf tail, long
Head Collar: White bucktail, short
Topping: Tan Fly Fur over head collar; pearl Krystal Flash
Eyes: 7mm or 10mm doll eyes
Modification: Pink topping over head collar

Half Hour Squid
(John Prigmore)

Hook: Mustad 34011; 2/0
Thread: White
Tail: Hackle (long), creme, cree; tan calf tail; pearl Flashabou
Body: Polar-fiber, tan, white; high-tied top, bottom, sides
Eyes: Marked mid-body with black marking pen

Crab Patterns

Lady Calico Merkin
(Del Brown)

Hook: Tiemco 811S; size 2/0
Thread: Orange Monocord, 3/0
Tail: Fluorescent orange Fluorofibre; ginger marabou
Body: Yarn, creme, orange; in alternating bands
Claws: Orange grizzly hackle (two), splayed
Legs: Round rubber legs, medium; banded with marker, red, black, tan
Eyes: Lead eyes

Pink Lady, large
(Alan Caolo)

Hook: Mustad 34011; 2/0-1/0
Thread: White
Tail: Hackle, pink, ginger grizzly; fluted
Body: Lead wire; gold poly braid
Wing: Hackle, pink, ginger grizzly; gold Krystal Flash
Collar: Pink rooster tail (very wide), palmered thick; dotted with brown marker
Eyes: Lead eyes, large; painted tan or bronze

Pink Lady, small
(Alan Caolo)

Hook: Mustad 34007/3407; size 1/0-1
Thread: White
Tail: Hackle, pink, creme; splayed
Body: Lead wire; white medium chenille
Wing: Pink hackle; gold Krystal Flash
Eyes: lead eyes; painted tan

Puglisi Crab Fly
(Enrico Puglisi)

Hook: Mustad 34007/3407; size 1-4
Thread: White
Tail: Tan Craft Fur; dark Krystal Flash
Body: Craft Fur, olive, tan; tied Merkin-style
Legs: Olive or brown flaked Sili-Legs
Eyes: Lead eyes, tied at hook bend
Modification: Trim legs to one half inch; additional lead eyes at hook eye

Green Crab Raghead
(Jan Isley)

Hook: Mustad 34007/3407; Tiemco 811S; size 1/0-1
Thread: Olive Monocord, 3/0
Tail: Navy blue Fluorofibre over chartreuse marabou
Body: Olive sheep fleece tied Merkin-style; saturated with contact cement
Claws: Olive grizzly hackle (two), splayed
Topping: Body dusted with olive wool
Legs: Round rubber legs, medium; banded with marker, blue, chartreuse, black
Eyes: Lead eyes

Chernobyl Crab
(Tim Borski/Umpqua Feather Merchants)

Hook: Mustad 34007; Tiemco 811S; size 1/0-2
Thread: White
Tail: Hot orange Krystal Flash; white calf tail; grizzly hackle
Body: Spun deer hair
Body Hackle: Wide hackle, grizzly or cree or badger; palmered
Weed Guard: Mason hard mono, 15#-20#
Eyes: Lead eyes, painted black on yellow on black

Shimmer-Leg Mole Crab
(Terry Baird)

Hook: Mustad 34007; size 1/0-4
Thread: White
Back: Gray Antron yarn or pearl poly braid
Body: Lead wire; medium chenille, white, orange (egg sac)
Legs: Clear/pearl silver-flake Sili-Legs
Claws: White hackle (tips)
Eyes: Plastic dumbbell or melted mono or bead chain
Modification: Back and body may be gray or tan or pale olive

Raghead Crab
(Jan Isley)

Hook: Owner 5106; size 3/0-1/0
Thread: Chartreuse
Tail: Tan marabou; tan hackle; pearl Krystal Flash
Body: Tan yarn; glue
Legs: White rubber legs
Eyes: Nickel-plated lead eyes

Simram
(Rick Simonson/Orvis Co.)

Hook: Mustad 34007; size 4-6
Thread: Danville's flat waxed nylon, pink
Tail: Craft Fur, light gold; yellow Krystal Flash, four strands
Body: Pearl Glitter Body; rabbit fur, tan, cross cut, notched on top
Eyes: Lead eyes, medium; painted tan or bronze

Chapter 5
Spotting the Fish

Fish spotting is an art. Those who are proficient at it often seem precognitive to those who are not. Anyone who's fished with a professional bonefish guide knows what I'm talking about. I vividly remember an afternoon on the water with Bonefish Joe Cleare of Harbour Island, Bahamas. As a way to test my spotting skills, I made a concerted effort to spot some fish that afternoon before Joe did. Over and over this man impressed me with how well he could see the fish. It wasn't long before I gave up measuring my own ability and just remained ready to look where this marvel said they would be. Being a young man (some 40 years younger than Joe) with good vision, how could this be? I later wondered how many bonefish would have swum by the skiff unnoticed had Joe not been there to point them out. Humbling as it was, this experience inspired me to work on my spotting skills and grow as an angler. Now, Joe is no ordinary man. One of the legendary bonefish guides, he was nearly 70 years young that day we fished together! Careful, well-camou-flaged fish on the flats are a bit like a tree that falls in the woods. How deserted those flats would have been for me had Bonefish Joe not been there to point them out.

Seeing fish in the water is an art of perception. Having 20-20 vision certainly doesn't hurt, but it is not nearly as relevant as knowing what to look for, where and how to look, and most importantly, how to interpret the cues that you physically see. Optometrists have convinced me that keen fish-spotting ability, like all sports vision concepts, is the result of a well-trained *mind*. An experienced angler processes visual images, translating a vague apparition into "Fish"!

Experience is the key. It is the rare individual who can board a flats skiff and teach the guide a lesson in spotting the quarry. A well-trained fish-spotting mind is the result of experience and practice. It takes time to learn all the visual signs of fish and how to interpret them. As always, there's no substitute for knowing your quarry. The ability to anticipate where stripers will appear and how they will be moving, based on the type of flat you're on, season, direction of water flow and structure, gives you that extra second or two to calmly make your presentation.

All successful flats-fishermen take the time to hone their spotting skills. The benefits of doing so are arithmetically simple—the more fish you see and the sooner you see them, results in a greater number of presentations you'll make, and the more hook-ups you'll get. Fishing with an experienced flats angler or guide from time to time will give you a good read as to how sharp you've become.

— How to Look —

When looking for fish you should always scan the water as opposed to focusing on one spot. By scanning, your eyes continually refocus and they won't become strained. It also helps you to pick up movement within your field of view. Since most visual cues you'll be looking for are based on movement, scanning is very important. The water should be scanned both in and out from your position as well as laterally across your field of view. This field should extend out only to the limits of where images may be perceived, and this will depend on several factors including sun position, water clarity, light level, ambient glare (resulting from haze, clouds, etc.), water surface condition, and your ability. Looking beyond your effective viewing range wastes time, strains your eyes, and leads to missed opportunities *within* your spotting range.

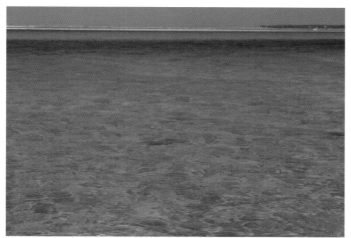

Looking into the water as you scan will reveal fish like this big one in the center of the picture.

Looking into the water, as opposed to across the surface, greatly improves how well you see the cues. Some high-tech glasses on the market today feature a vertically polarized gradient within the eyepiece, allowing you to adjust the level of polarization (and the amount of light received by your eyes) by simply dipping or raising your head slightly. This allows you to quickly refine how well you see images below the water surface by reducing the glare or by adding light to your view.

You should be aware that small surface waves on the water change the angles of incident and reflected light. This allows you to easily peer through the water and pick up underwater images much more clearly. A profound example of this is the superb view you get when looking down the curl of a wave as it approaches the beach. Here, advancing stripers may be clearly spotted several hundred feet down the beach by progressively looking along the wave as it rolls in. When light conditions are good and the waves are smooth and well defined, expansive beaches may be covered rapidly using this technique without any missed opportunities.

Waves simplify spotting fish in the surf.

About the Sun and Sky

A great deal of your ability to see the fish depends on the atmospheric conditions of sun and sky. A blue sky with bright sun is ideal and the further overhead the sun is, the better. Of course, optimum viewing prevails with the sun at your back. During morning and afternoon fishing in the Northeast the viewing becomes constrained to one direction much more than in the tropics. This is due to a reduced solar declination angle, or simply put, the sun is lower in the sky resulting in less light intensity. As a result, the duration of premium viewing each day is shorter than in the tropics.

CHART C3
Comparison of Maximum Solar Declination

	Southern New England Latitude N41° 22′	Islamorada Latitude N24° 55′
June 1st	70.7°	87.2°
July 1st	71.6°	87.7°
August 1st	66.6°	82.7°
September 1st	56.9°	73.2°
October 1st	46.6°	61.7°

It should also be noted that the period of daily viewing shortens considerably due to the seasonal reduction in solar declination as fall approaches. For anglers, this means that optimum viewing may be expected during the months of June and July where high-quality light prevails from 9:00 a.m. to about 5:00 p.m. The duration of high-quality viewing diminishes quickly during the latter half of the sight-fishing season to six hours by mid-September, from about 10:00 a.m. to 4:00 p.m.

A white sky creates a water surface riddled with glare that makes spotting difficult.

Fog provides filtered light and a dark backdrop that create excellent viewing.

Puffy, white cumulus clouds that turn the lights on and off require patience.

The sky is the other important factor in determining the quality of daily viewing. The sky as a backdrop governs the level of glare (scattered light) cast from the water's surface. A dark sky or blue sky provides a nice backdrop, which creates very little glare and high visibility prevails. A white sky (stratus or cirrostratus clouds), on the other hand, produces the opposite condition by creating a water surface riddled with glare and very difficult to penetrate with our mortal vision.

The impact of these facts may seem obvious, but they are subtle. Here's why: a great summer day can be hot, sunny and bright, and it may seem that spotting conditions will be perfect. But moisture in the air, known as haze, creates a white sky and the spotting may be tougher than you thought. A dark overcast day (or fog), on the other hand, may seem lousy for sight-fishing, but it is not. The glare-free surface allows easy viewing and the fish may be readily spotted at short to medium distances. I'll take a dark overcast or foggy day over a bright white hazy day any time.

Frontal clouds may tarnish your view when looking in their direction.

Also keep in mind that high white frontal clouds (altocumulus) or white clouds on the horizon (cumulus) in the direction in which you are looking may temporarily hamper your view, even on an otherwise blue-sky day with lots of sun. Though these clouds do not occlude the sun, their reflection off the water can create formidable glare. Patience pays here, but sometimes it is better to adjust your viewing direction slightly to avoid the white backdrop and improve the spotting, even though the sun may no longer be directly at your back, until the clouds clear from your viewing field.

Partly cloudy days generally produce stop-and-go fishing conditions as cirrus or cumulus clouds intermittently block the sun, effectively "turning off the lights". When these conditions prevail, I find it's best to stop moving until the cloud clears and the lights come on again. Fewer unseen fish are spooked this way, improving overall daily success.

Visual Cues

A variety of visual cues reveal striped bass. With good viewing and the right glasses, clear images of the fish (stripes and all) may be observed. In bright conditions the fish will appear golden brown; with fog or a dark overcast sky (nimbus or cumulonimbus) the fish will appear bluish gray and very phantom-like. Many times the striper's mirror-like sides fade from view, leaving only the fish's back visible. Here, even though the fish itself is observed, the narrow appearance of the back alone can be deceiving, especially when viewed coming head-on. More often, however, anglers see moving shadows or indistinct grayish or bluish images.

An experienced angler picks up subtle contrasts and movement and the trained mind fills in the rest. The striper's shadow appearance varies according to the water depth, light intensity, and how far above the bottom the fish is swimming. The brighter the light and shallower the water the darker and more well defined the shadow becomes. Most times it appears as a hazy, elongate shape.

Other times it may be dark and well defined, and still other times it may appear as nothing more than an ill-defined, faint-gray moving blotch. If you're unsure of what to look for at any time, take a quick look at the appearance of your own shadow on the flat bottom to calibrate your mind. In any event, the image may be confirmed as a fish with the detection or sensation of movement. Bass rarely lie motionless on a flat (and when they do their bellies are on the bottom and they cast no shadow), so if it doesn't change position it's not a fish.

A technique I use when spotting fish over broken or mottled bottoms is to focus on relative movement. Looking for objects that are moving or changing position relative to ones that are fixed is effective for detecting fish over difficult bottoms. Weed patches, rocks and other visible stationary features make good reference points. When there is tidal movement or flow, any elongate image advancing *against* the tide is certainly an obvious cue.

Flashes off the sides of stripers are another image to look for. This occurs when large bass roll as they pick something off the bottom and devour it (they also roll near the bottom to shed parasites such, as sea lice, in the spring). The sight is exciting, as the fish send off a chromium flash that always makes them seem larger than they already are.

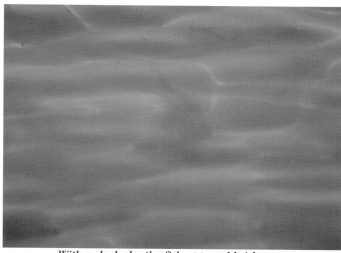

With a dark sky the fish appear bluish gray.

Flashes effectively reveal fish with marginal viewing conditions and at distances that they would otherwise not be spotted.

Stripers occasionally exhibit bonefish-like behavior and

Only the back and shadow of this well-adjusted striper remain visible in bright sun.

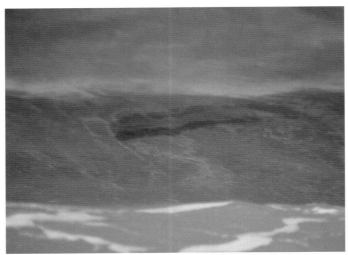

With bright sun and shallow water the striper's shadow appears crisp and dark.

This striper just about has his belly on the bottom and casts no shadow.

"wake" or "tail" while on the flats, but unfortunately this exciting way of spotting fish occurs too infrequently to be relied upon on a daily basis. One reason is simply that stripers prefer deeper water than bonefish do. Another is that the majority of food that bonefish eat resides within the bottom whereby rooting and tailing are routine feeding strategies for bones. Stripers tail from time to time when feeding on crabs, shrimp or flounder in shallow water, however they rarely stay in that feeding posture for long. Waking fish are easily spotted by the nervous water they create, or a surface push that contrasts with the adjacent water. Stripers generally roam water shallow enough to create wakes (15 inches deep, or less) during first-light conditions that are often accompanied by little or no wind and a glassy surface, which facilitates seeing these surface cues.

How to Interpret the Cues

Taking a moment to carefully examine the images of the fish will provide significant information. Instead of immediately firing off casts, I recommend that anglers analyze what they've seen and then make the presentation. With experience, you'll know right away how to handle each fish.

First, note the shade of the fish. Like most game fish, stripers' skin coloration changes to suit their surroundings. When coming from deep water or non-sand-bottom locations, they may appear quite dark as they embark on the flats. Fish that have been on the sand for a while lighten up considerably to blend with their surroundings. As a result, dark fish (or "fresh fish") tend to be hungrier, more aggressive, and more likely to take a fly. Pale fish that have

Stripers do tail occasionally in shallow water, but not for as long as bonefish will.

Fish tipped down 45 degrees to the bottom are excellent slow-moving targets.

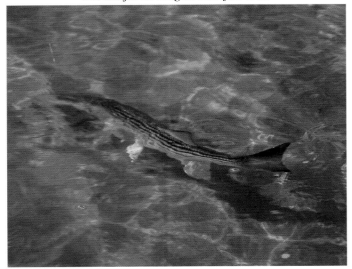

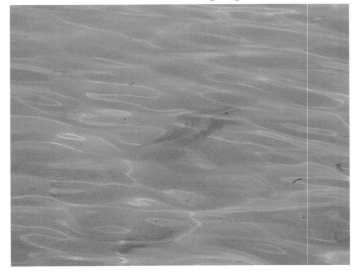

Note how far the shadow is offset from the body of this high-riding fish.

been on the flats for a while are more in tune with the flat's environment and may be a bit tougher to interest with a fly. Coloration changes occur in about an hour or two.

Also note the fish's shadow position. If you can see the fish itself and its shadow appears substantially offset from its body, then you know it is swimming high. Such fish are either in transit or are feeding up on baitfish. These fish are most effectively taken with high-riding up flies. Fish with small shadows, cast very near their bodies, are most certainly on the bottom. Here, weighted, bottom-working flies are best.

Rolling stripers are almost always actively feeding on the bottom. These fish are very good targets and are best presented with weighted, deep-working flies. These fish are often eating crabs and I've had much success with crab flies on flashing fish. The fish turn on their sides to permit the mouth to extend fully open, making best use of the vacuum effect created as they inhale difficult-to-catch bottom prey. The gills are often flared in the process, making the event exciting for anglers to witness.

Stripers may hold in the flow of shallow channels or on flats with moderate currents. Once they've adjusted their color, these non-moving fish can be very hard to spot. Shadow forms which subtly materialize out of nowhere and them mysteriously evaporate without a trace are a telltale sign of holding fish. What is happening is the fish are revealed only when they rise slightly off the bottom, creating a shadow, as they capture incoming prey. As the fish settles back to the bottom, the shadow goes away. These fish are best approached with small flies that are cast ahead of the fish and dead drifted, or gently twitched into the fish's hold. Oftentimes these fish are feeding on shrimp.

Fish observed tipped down as they drift with the tide, or clearly tailing head down as they root about with their mouths in the sand, are foraging on burrowing prey. Crabs, shrimp, flounder and sand eels are all possible food sources. Here, carefully placed bottom-working flies that are mildly retrieved work best. Briskly stripped flies and high-riding up flies often startle these fish, which are intensely focused on the bottom.

Glasses and Hats

To effectively see the visual cues you'll be looking for, you'll need the right polarized sunglasses. I recommend owning more than one pair for several reasons. First, no one pair of glasses, no matter what the cost or quality, can meet all of your needs, all of the time. There are some good "compromise" lenses available today that meet many of the demands of flats fishing, but they are a compromise, and often they do not satisfy the needs of unique spotting conditions. Second, sunglasses are perhaps second only to rod-tips on the list of equipment casualties suffered both on and off the water each year. Owning more than one pair of glasses allows you to stay on the water and continue fishing in such an event. I recommend owning at least one pair of high-quality sunglasses for all-around general-purpose flats work, and some inexpensive pairs to cover special conditions. When you consider the importance of having the right glasses while sight-fishing, $200 for three pairs is a minor investment, especially when compared to the cost of rods and reels today.

Polarized sunglasses perform several functions that assist your vision and help you spot your quarry. All of them should be considered when purchasing your glasses, and later when using them on the flats. These functions include reducing light levels, reducing glare, filtering out certain colors and improving contrast.

First, the amount of tint in the lens determines the level of light that reaches your eyes. On bright days, dark lenses provide comfort and ease eyestrain. With low-light conditions, associated with early morning, fog or dark overcast skies, a lighter tint admits more light, providing a better view. What is unique about flats fishing is that the objects we look for and the background we look against are both light-colored. On the flats, even the brightest of days do not call for extremely dark lenses and a medium-tint amber lens is ideal. Very dark lenses foul the flats-fisherman's view by admitting so little light that many of the subtle images we look for become no longer visible. Low light transmission also causes your pupils to dilate. The acuity, or sharpness, of our vision is best when the pupil is contracted, which enables sharp focusing. This fine-tuning is lost somewhat with dark glasses. The medium tint provided by most brown- or amber-colored lenses is ideal for the brightest flats-fishing conditions.

Polarized glasses come in varying degrees of polarization and therefore provide varying degrees of glare reduction. Glare results from horizontally scattered light that has

A blue sky with bright sun creates ideal viewing. Note the fish surfing the zone.

been reflected by the water's surface, or by moisture in the atmosphere, such as fog and haze. The reduction of glare is important to viewing below the water's surface and to relax your vision and prevent fatigue. In general, the darker a lens' tint, the greater the level of polarization.

Some manufacturers of high-quality glasses, such as Maui Jim and Action Optics, offer a multi-function composite lens construction. In addition to blocking 100% of harmful ultraviolet radiation, these glasses provide excellent glare reduction from above and below, as well as straight into your eyes without heavily tinting the lens. Inexpensive glasses do not perform as well and your viewing will not be as good, however, certain manufacturers, such as Flying Fisherman offer very high value. These glasses lack the style and super performance of the high-end products but they are excellent fishing glasses, they are well made (with glass lenses) and they cost under $20.

Lens color is very important, it admits certain colors and filters out others, thus narrowing the color range in your field of view. Contrast within that color band is also greatly enhanced. All game fish that operate on the flats are either endowed with coloration that provides the necessary camouflage, or they are able to modify their appearance to blend with their surroundings, as bonefish and stripers do so well. A lens tint similar to the bottom color greatly improves contrast and fish are spotted much more easily. The fish themselves, as well as the shadows they cast, become more visible and stand out against the light background. Medium amber is ideal for spotting stripers over sand in bright light conditions. With diminishing light levels, pale amber works best to admit more light and maintain contrast on overcast or hazy days. With good light and a grass or otherwise dark bottom, medium and pale brown tints work well as they pick up faint shadows well over the dark bottom. With low light levels over grass or dark sand, a bright yellow tint works wonders. Here, the bright tint admits lots of light so that faint visual images become strong and contrast is maximized. Yellow lenses are also recommended for foggy or dark overcast days as contrast is substantially improved. As a final point on lens color, all glasses for sight-fishing should be in the brown-amber-yellow spectrum to match the bottom color. Blue, gray and green lens tints, ideal for bluewater fishing, should be avoided.

With regard to frames and lens materials, I recommend a wrap-around style with glass lenses as the best combination. Plastic or polycarbonate lenses scratch easily and are easily broken. They are lighter and more comfortable over the course of a day's fishing, but the long-lasting durability of glass is more important in the long run. Having a lightweight pair or two might not be a bad idea if you own several pairs, however,.

Wrap-style frames minimize the reflection of sunlight off the *inside* of the lens that distorts your focus and causes eye fatigue; both degrade viewing. Since sight-fishers scan the water with the sun primarily at their backs, sunlight can easily strike the inside surface of the lenses by entering from behind and from the sides. Wraps close off this opening and improve your view by allowing the pupil to dilate somewhat to best suit the light levels of the images coming in through the lens.

Non-wrap-style glasses may be easily fit with flexible side-shields that slide over the earpiece and mold into position adjacent to the frames. They are inexpensive and work very well. Recently, polarized goggle-type glasses, intended for other water sports such as jet skiing, have appeared on the market. I have tried them and they are the ultimate eyewear for preventing back-glare as they completely enclose the eye socket and upper cheek. I suspect that in the years to come, this style of eyewear will become the standard for serious flats-fishers. Though they may appear a little strange, goggles are the superior frame design and they are far less bizarre than many other items routinely worn by fly-fishers today.

A good all-around selection of glasses for flats fishing would consist of three unique pairs. Since bright light and light-shaded bottoms are encountered often while sight-fishing stripers (as well as the tropics), one high-quality pair with glass, medium-amber lenses is a must. I would also include a pair of yellow-lens glasses for grass bottoms and low light conditions. A pair of pale amber or pale brown lenses would round out the set for hazy and high overcast days. For days with highly variable sun, or when working over a variably shaded bottom (grass and sand, for example), two pairs of glasses can be quickly interchanged to suit the situation by keeping your glasses around your neck on lanyards or Croakies.

Hats are the other important piece of fish-spotting equipment. They are also vital to provide protection from harmful ultraviolet sunlight. Hats come in as many styles as there are people. For sight-fishing, the only requirement is that the hat have a large, wide frontal bill, or brim, to shade your eyes and keep the sun off your face. The underside of the brim should be dark and dull to minimize reflection of light off the water from bouncing back down off the underside of the bill and into your eyes. A dark brim absorbs this light, further enhancing your vision and allowing sunglasses to perform better. A light under-brim can be darkened with a colored marker, and a glossy or plastic one can be dulled with a Scotch Pad.

Chapter 6

Presentation and Retrieve

❧✦❧

As with all flats fishing, fly presentation and retrieve are critical to success. Sight-fishing is more demanding than other forms of saltwater fly-fishing because of the suddeness with which things happen on the flats and the lack of choice as to how you may respond. Sight-casters must consistently make fast, accurate casts to moving targets. They must do this on cue with whatever the wind is doling out at the time. Furthermore, they start their casts with fly-in-hand where getting the cast going and loading the rod quickly in response to the sudden presence of large game fish can test your nerve.

These elements of sight-fishing elevate fly-fishers to the next level. You'll rarely hear a seasoned bonefisher complain about wind or the suddenness with which anything happens while fishing. The wind has become a friend and sudden, one-shot opportunities at trophy game fish are the lifeblood of a thrilling addiction. Very little rattles them on the flats or in any other angling situation.

Presentation and retrieve are the physical aspects of an otherwise entirely cerebral sport. Grand casting ability is a wonderful asset, but it is worthless if it can't be executed when it counts. When equipped with nerves of steel and an ability to see the fish reasonably well, less-than-average casters will consistently out-fish superior casters who do not share the same thirst for excitement. No one manages a perfect scorecard on the flats, however. When an opportunity is fumbled, the sight-fisher's angling spirit is not dampened. Whatever can be gleaned from the experience is tucked away for the future and the next thrilling opportunity is anxiously awaited. Each sight-fishing hook-up is a very gratifying moment.

— Sight-Casting Fundamentals —

A prerequisite for quality presentation is that you have maintained your stealth and not alerted the fish to your presence. Moving slowly and quietly while wading or poling in a skiff allows you to get within casting range of more fish. Make every effort to avoid hard contact with the hull of the skiff, either with feet, tackle or the pole. Such conspicuous noises are efficiently radiated from fiberglass hulls as underwater vibration, which stripers readily detect. These vibrations travel far and fast in seawater (especially in shallow water) and alert stripers well away from the skiff. A lightfooted approach while wading that minimizes hard contact with the bottom or bank and avoids water surface noise (sloshing, etc.), will also get you closer to far more fish.

As always, reducing to a low profile while retrieving the fly will preserve your stealth. Staying low after the cast should become second nature while sight-casting to striped bass. The inconspicuous attire and the rod and line treatments described in Chapter Eight will greatly improve your stealth, creating opportunities for many more fish, even at very close range.

Stripers are sometimes spotted well beyond casting range, which gives anglers plenty of time to get the cast going and plan the presentation. But more often, they first appear already within range and they're often moving quickly. To make the quick casts necessary for these fish, anglers should practice winding up from a "ready position" that allows accurate casts of 30 to 70 feet to be made with three false casts or less. Once you find a system that works and you are comfortable with it, you should use it consistently to refine the motions to the point where getting the cast off becomes mindless second nature. Fly lines can be

Crouching low during the retrieve effectively removes the angler from the fish's view.

The same ready position used from a skiff is ideal when posted-up on shore.

conveniently marked with a waterproof pen at familiar lengths to help anglers gauge distance and become consistent technical casters through practice and time on the water. I use two different ready positions—one for skiff-fishing or while posted-up on shore, and another for wading or walking the shoreline.

The Ready Position From Skiffs and Shore-Banks

From a skiff, anglers are usually positioned to cast from the bow deck where effective casts may be made over nearly 360 degrees. To get started, the angler stands at this bow position and strips from the reel only the amount of line that can be comfortably cast with the wind conditions at hand. If the viewing is limited, this line should be shortened to suit the reduced range. Using a line length only as long as needed to make presentations with the conditions at hand

Getting ready. The shooting line is laid on the deck in loose coils away from feet and deck features.

minimizes the risk of excess line fouling on the deck (or shoreline entanglements), becoming wind-blown and tangled, or being stepped on while casting. Any of these events ruin opportunities and lead to frustration. A minimal line also has less chance of fouling while clearing the line after a striper has been hooked. The line is then straightened by stretching it with your hands in four-foot increments until all the memory coils have been removed. With the line straight and manageable, the angler casts out a suitable distance and then strips in the line letting it lay on the deck in large, loose coils away from feet and deck features.

The fly is held by the bend of the hook between the thumb and forefinger of the line-hand with the leader and 10 to 15 feet of fly line out of the rod-tip. From this position the rod may be loaded quickly to get a cast off easily in any direction with as few false casts as possible. With the fish spotted, the cast is started by making a roll cast aimed above the water in the direction of the target while the fly is released from the line-hand. By shooting a little line on the backcast the entire line head can be airborne in a single false cast. When properly executed, the rod is loaded and the angler is ready to shoot the fly to the fish in two or three false casts. The long length of fly line out of the tip also allows short casts of 25 feet or less to be made simply by rolling this line out to the target. A stripping basket may be used as an alternative, but they can impede quick maneuvering on a skiff, they prohibit crouching low on the retrieve from the shore and they are not recommended.

The Ready Position While Wading

Presentation distances are shorter while wading and sufficient line may be carried in long coils in the fingers of your rod-hand as you wade. Again, strip only enough line off the reel to cast a comfortable distance within your viewing range. For most conditions this is about 50 feet from the rod-tip (50 feet of fly line off the reel with a nine-foot rod and a 10-foot leader). This may shorten to 30 or even 20 feet with marginal viewing conditions. With about eight to 10 feet of

A ready position for wade fishing.

Where to Place the Fly

The objective of every sight-casting presentation is the same: *to present the fly with a cast that places it sufficiently ahead of the fish to allow it to sink to the depth that the fish is feeding prior to the start of the retrieve. Further, position the fly so that its distance from the fish is increasing as it is retrieved.* There are some subtle differences between this description of an ideal presentation and those you may have read in the past. As you shall see, this presentation concept allows the flexibility to capitalize on more opportunities and it eliminates common errors made while sight-fishing.

CHART C4

Presentation Leads in Feet

Fish Speed	Water Depth in Feet			
	1-2	2-3	3-4	4-5
Slow	6	8	10	12
Moderate	8	12	15	20
Fast	10	15	20	25

Placing the fly far enough ahead to allow it to reach the fish's level before bringing it to life enhances the presentation. It's best if the fly reaches this position well before the fish closes to within range of seeing it. The start of the retrieve is carefully timed so that the fly is moving and appearing quite natural when it is first spotted. Starting the retrieve too early, however, may draw the fly out of the zone before the fish is in range of seeing it. Starting it too late appears unnatural and can startle your quarry.

FLY PLACEMENT

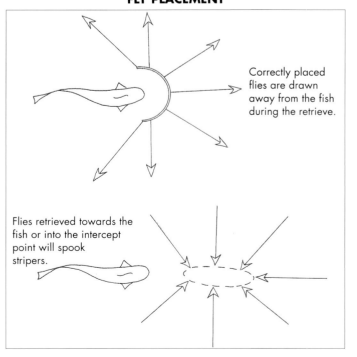

Correctly placed flies are drawn away from the fish during the retrieve.

Flies retrieved towards the fish or into the intercept point will spook stripers.

fly line out of the rod-tip, the fly is held by the bend of the hook between the thumb and forefinger of the line-hand. The remaining shooting line is held in the ring and little fingers of your rod-hand in large, loose, three-foot-diameter coils. With this set-up, the rod is easily loaded with the long length of fly line already out past the tip and casts of 20 to 50 feet may be made quickly.

When a fish is spotted, a quick roll cast and simultaneous release of the fly gets the cast going. Adequate line to load the rod is fed through the guides while false casting. When properly executed, the angler should be able to shoot whatever is necessary to get the fly to the fish with three false casts or less. After the cast is made, the unused shooting line is simply dropped into the water as the fly is retrieved. Clearing this line is rarely a problem and there is little chance of it fouling on the tangle-free sand bottom. This technique requires some practice to get used to and it may not be best for everyone. If not, I emphasize that anglers develop a comfortable scheme that works to make fast, accurate presentations throughout one's casting range, and use it consistently.

Nothing in the wild waits until a predator is on the doorstep to jump out of hiding and flee. In order to survive, prey either run for cover early or stay still when it's too late to move when predators are near. To freeze or flee is certainly a precarious decision for prey. When surprised by a predator they sometimes make their move too late and the big fish gets fed. The key here is that the predator surprises the prey and not the other way around. As a sight-fisher, this is the natural drama you strive to mimic with your presentation whether your quarry is striped bass, bonefish, permit or tarpon. Everything must appear natural and unfold as it does in the wild. A complete lack of response to the fly, positive or negative, misleads many beginners to think that the fly is of no interest to the fish. Any striper that shows absolutely no response to a presentation has not seen the fly. It takes experience and a good sense of where your fly is in the water to master this part of the game.

The Retrieve

Aside from when to start it, a retrieve consists of two elements: its speed and its cadence. The speed of the retrieve should suit the size and speed of the fish you're casting to. Most often, large and trophy-sized stripers move rather slowly while feeding and a slow retrieve works best for these slow pokes. Other times, slow-moving fish are reluctant to follow a fly and only a fly placed right in their path that is barely twitched will entice them. Small stripers, under 10 pounds, generally swim more quickly and sometimes move erratically while feeding—much like bonefish. These fish will readily chase down a fly and a brisk retrieve works well on them. But most importantly, the speed of the retrieve should suit the speed of the fish, regardless of its size.

The cadence of the retrieve should impart the natural action of the prey being imitated. Squid evade predators with a darting fashion. Here, a snappy 12-inch strip retrieve appears natural and is effective. Shrimp and most baitfish are well imitated with a tempered, steady strip retrieve that suits the speed of the fish. Shrimp and juvenile flounder are frequently carried with the tide and a drag-free dead drift works wonders in a shallow channel current. Immobile prey, such as worms, require no stripping. Here, barely twitching the fly and letting the water movement do the rest makes an effective presentation. A perfectly placed worm pattern that is subsequently stripped will appear so unnatural that stripers will flee from it. Mole crab patterns are also interesting since they require movement to work, but anglers must not retrieve them. Instead, they are presented in a surf current, which rolls them over the bottom, just like the natural.

It is important that the retrieve is *steady*. I find that motionless flies and erratic, stop-and-go retrieves that are effective on bonefish and permit fail to entice stripers most of the time. The fly should be moving, whether by stripping, twitching or by natural water movement. Once a fish is following, speeding up or slowing down the cadence generally does little to draw a strike. The striper is following because it likes what it sees. Keep a steady cadence and let the fish decide when it wants to eat—it can't be force-fed.

— Casting Considerations —

Casting skill is essential for successful sight-fishing. Some fly-casters place a lot of emphasis on the appearance of their cast and on distance. For sight-casters, the priorities should be accuracy, consistency, speed of delivery, distance and smoothness of delivery—in that order.

The Basics

These casting objectives combine to make sight-casting more challenging than blind-casting, where timing and wind considerations are much less important. And there is the visual element as well. Sight-casters must do what they do by responding to a quarry that may have been stalked for hours and is now clearly in view, but offers just a glimpse of an opportunity.

Experienced sight-fishers seize the moment. An entire event can occur, from start to finish, in less time than it takes a blind-caster to light a cigarette. I wish I was able to capture with words the rush that addicted sight-fishers experience when they encounter their quarry, it can easily cause opportunities to be fumbled. Controlling this excitement is difficult, but learning to manage it through your presentation will enable you to enjoy an even more thrilling experience, a take!

While there are no substitutes for practice and experience on the water for developing sight-casting skills, understanding a few basics will help immensely. The best casting accuracy is achieved with an over-the-shoulder motion. By looking at your target and casting with a vertical stroke, much more accurate casts are possible than with the rod angled to the side or with a full sidearm motion. Most baseball pitchers and football quarterbacks throw overhand for the same reason.

Consistency and speed of delivery are developed through practice. High-performance equipment, lessons, books and videos help but practice is the key. Golf is a game of consistency and most good golfers I know practice a heck of a lot. For sight-casters, loading the rod and delivering the cast quickly is very important. Practicing with as long a line out of the rod-tip as possible will help. Working with a long line is tough at first, but once you're comfortable managing a long line out of the tip, the speed with which you load the rod with a roll cast start-up will improve dramatically. I like 15 to 20 feet for skiff fishing and 10 to 12 feet for wading.

Distance and smoothness of delivery are realized by using your tackle efficiently and through timing. Fly rods are nothing more than springs. The mass of the fly line bends the spring, effectively loading it, as you go through your casting motion. Casting energy is effectively transferred to the fly line through a well-timed casting cadence. As the rod flexes, it stores energy that is released at the end of your speed-up and stop cast-stroke. There is no need to swing the rod powerfully as you cast. Good, smooth timing will generate a good deal of rod bending that effectively loads the rod with stored energy necessary to propel the cast. Let the *rod* do the work. With a firm grip, this energy transfers efficiently to the line launching it with a smooth, well-formed loop as the rod unloads.

The Double Haul

Greater distance is achieved as line speed and the length of line in the air while false casting increases. Since carrying a lot of line in the air makes casting in the wind progressively more difficult, I recommend improving distance by using the double haul, which greatly increases line speed. The wind is almost always blowing on the flats and the double haul is much easier for most people than handling a lot of airborne fly line. Well-timed double hauling, with only the line's head out of the rod-tip, enables accurate casts to be made at long distances, where a long line flailing in the wind does not. Double hauling effectively adds momentum to the fly line, which helps cut through the wind (regardless of its direction) considerably. This is a great asset even when casting short distances.

The double haul is executed by simply pulling down on the line a short distance with the line-hand as the rod is swept through the power stroke. This is done on both the forward cast and the backcast with short six- to twelve-inch pulls on the line. The length of the pull need not be longer than this to further load the rod and add speed to the line. Longer hauls can create slack in the line, complicate timing, cause reel-wrap (when the line loops around the reel or the rod butt), and are simply not necessary to make the double haul work. The line-hand should follow the rod grip as the haul is made during the backcast so that it will be close to the reel and ready to pull slack-free line at the start of the forward cast. The line-hand should move down and away from the reel during the forward haul. As double-haul proficiency is gained and timing improves, the haul may be made with faster pulls of the line during the power strokes to add even more line speed and greater distance.

The double haul increases distance and helps cut through the wind on short casts.

The Reach Cast

The reach cast is simple to execute. With a normal forward cast the fly is delivered toward the target. As the line is progressing through the air at the end of the delivery stroke, the rod is gradually tilted to the side as you extend your reach in that direction. The rod should be fully horizontal with your arms extended as the fly touches down at the target. The reach cast can be executed with or without shooting any line, but in either case it's most effective at ranges of 40 feet or less.

The Curve Cast

Curve casts are the most difficult sight-fishing casts to make. Their effectiveness, however, makes them worthwhile to practice. The following descriptions of left and right curve casts apply to right-handed casters. Left-handed casters need only reverse these descriptions intuitively.

A left curve is made with an overpowered sidearm cast that is aimed *over the target*. The extra power causes the fly and leader to hook to the left creating a curve in the presentation as the fly line falls to the water. A stiff leader butt will help the curve form.

A right curve is difficult and works for most people only about half the time. A sidearm casting stroke is again used, except the cast is now underpowered. The curve is formed by gently sweeping an arc with the rod. The slow line speed and resulting weak cast lose momentum and fall to the water before the wide casting loop has completely rolled straight. Now, a limp leader helps the curve to form. When executed correctly, the fly line and leader form a curve to the right.

The sidearm delivery and the nature of underpowering and overpowering these casts limit both left and right curves to a short effective range of about 35 feet or less. There are other more advanced methods of achieving a curve, but they are very difficult and are beyond the scope of this book.

Pile and Wiggle Casts

Two simple techniques provide controlled slack in the cast, which is important to create free-float in the fly line for dead-drift presentations. Pile and wiggle casts are ideal for accomplishing this when presenting to fish down current when the fly must drift to them and not drag, hold or swing in the current. Both are easy to execute.

The wiggle cast is accomplished by making a normal cast to the target, but with about 10 feet of extra line in the cast. With the cast-loop unfolding and the fly heading to the target, the rod-tip is wiggled side-to-side as it is extended to the target. The wider the side-to-side motion, the more built-in slack will be created. As the fly line falls to the water, a series of wiggles form in the line, which consume the extra 10 feet of line and create controlled slack in the cast. The fly may now free-float down-current for several feet to the holding fish before the line comes tight.

The pile cast accomplishes the same result with a different technique. Here, a normal cast is made, again with about 10 feet of extra line to provide the slack. As the fly is delivered to the target and the loop is unfolding, the rod tip is suddenly dropped all the way to the water. The fly line close to the angler is forced to the water too early, which zaps the cast of its energy and the remaining airborne line fails to straighten and falls to the water in a heap up-current of the target. A wide-open casting loop accomplishes this best. The fly may now free-float down-current to the fish as the pile of fly line straightens out.

The Sidearm Cast

When casting to fish at short range on bright flats, stealth can be greatly improved by using a sidearm cast, which suppresses rod-flash considerably. I recommend a low casting angle for presenting the fly at ranges of 30 feet or less, especially when gloss-finished rods are used. The sidearm cast is nothing more than a normal cast made with the rod angled to the side. With fish at very close range the rod should be angled as low as possible using a flat cast-stroke, parallel to the water. A powerful stroke keeps the line airborne with good line speed. A weak cast-stroke may cause the line, which is just inches above the water, to strike the surface and spook the fish.

The Roll Cast Startup

Successful sight-casting depends on a good start-up from a ready position that is initiated with a well-executed roll cast. A good roll cast is made by bringing the rod fully back to a 10 o'clock position with the rod-hand positioned at eye-level and the rod cocked in the position typical of the start of a normal forward cast. Driving the rod forward now, as with a normal forward cast, while releasing the fly with your line-hand gets the line moving briskly in the vertical plane and puts the fly airborne in one stroke. An arcing motion with the rod generates weak line speed causing the fly to fall downward and should be avoided. Aiming the roll cast high sets the cast in motion much more effectively. With one cast, everything is in motion *up in the air* where successive false casts will build line speed and direct the delivery.

Overcoming the Wind

The wind will be with you on the flats far more often than not, and learning to deal with it, eventually utilizing it to your advantage, is the hallmark of every successful sight-fisher. I consider air movement below five knots to be windless as far as casting is concerned. Above that velocity your casting can be adjusted to suit the conditions until wind speeds of 20 knots are reached, when it's time to leave the flats. The four basic wind casts encountered are: a head-wind, a tail-wind, a cross-wind into your casting shoulder, and a cross-wind away from your casting shoulder.

Head-winds are tough but with the right technique they become easier than tail-winds. Since the wind is blowing back your cast, using a high backcast will take advantage of this. Let the wind fully extend your backcast by holding it for a second or two before coming forward. This really helps load the rod on the forward cast. Now, a smooth forward stroke that aims the fly *down to the target* and follows through with an extended reach-out will make full use of the rod's power and direct the fly and fly line to the water, not

above it as with most other casts. The most common mistake made with a head-wind is trying to overpower the cast.

Tail-winds wreak havoc with backcasts by blowing them forward and preventing full line extension. Weakened backcasts have slack and are not straight, making strong forward casts difficult to execute. The rod is simply not loaded effectively. Tail-winds call for a modified approach. Instead of keeping a high backcast, as we're accustomed to doing with other casts, tail-winds call for a low backcast. Wind speeds are lower near the ground and backcasts thrown at low trajectories cut through the wind better and fully extend. The forward cast is smoothly made with a slight upward trajectory, allowing the wind to help carry the fly to the target. Here, the backcast must be made powerfully—haul it hard.

A cross-wind away from your casting shoulder is the easiest of the wind casts to handle and no special techniques are called for, other than increasing line speed by double hauling. The wind will blow the cast away from the target, but a well-executed double haul helps keep the cast on target by driving it through the wind. Depending on the wind velocity, some degree of cross-wind effect will occur which can be offset by aiming the cast to the windward side of the target by an appropriate amount. When time permits, some anglers test-fire a cast in the general direction of the fish they're targeting to get a read on the wind's effect, then pick up and shoot a calibrated cast to the target.

A cross-wind into your casting shoulder is unquestionably the toughest. Not only does this wind blow the fly off course, it pushes the airborne fly line into the angler and guide, putting both at risk of being hit by the fly. Fortunately, there are three ways to handle this wind. The simplest involves merely turning about face and delivering the fly on your backcast, which is now safely downwind. The advantage here is ease and simplicity. The disadvantage is that you are not looking at your target as you make the cast, and backcasts are typically not accurate to begin with. Like taking your eye off the opening when making a hockey wrist shot—you'll hit the net, but it probably won't go exactly where you want.

The second method is to use a sidearm cast. A sidearm casting stroke will push the fly and fly line away from the angler and into the wind and the cast must be made powerfully with an incoming cross-wind. The advantages here are that you can continue to look at your target as you make the cast. Though sidearm casts are less accurate than casting overhead, this method is better than throwing on the backcast. The sidearm cast is made low to the water where there is much less wind velocity and the accuracy of the delivery cast is much less affected by cross-wind effect. A disadvantage here is that this cast must be made powerfully and it requires practice (in the wind) to perfect it. Also, when fishing on a skiff the guide or your partner may be positioned upwind of you making the sidearm a bad choice in this situation.

The third means of coping with this wind is to angle the rod over the downwind shoulder as the cast is made, thus allowing the fly and fly line to pass safely downwind of you as you false cast. This method requires a slightly different casting rhythm, which takes some practice to develop, however, it is very accurate and easy to execute once you've learned it. In fact, the harder the cross-wind blows, the easier and better this method becomes.

— Basic Presentations —

Nearly every situation encountered while stalking stripers can be handled with one of five basic presentations. Each is effective on inshore flats, offshore flats and in the surf. On some days all five techniques may be called for, particularly when the visibility is good and the flat you're fishing holds many fish. But more often the quality of the viewing, the nature of the flat you're fishing and the striper's feeding patterns cause specific casting situations to recur, calling for certain presentations again and again. The most frequently encountered situations call for head-on or perpendicular presentations.

Head-on Presentations

A common casting angle is head-on to the fish. With good sun and high visibility, anglers can spot fish well out of casting range and readily position themselves for a head-on shot. By head-on I am referring to any casting angle within 30 degrees of dead ahead. Wider casting angles should be considered perpendicular presentation.

Here, the fly is placed in front of advancing fish no more than four feet to either side of the fish's track to ensure it's within their field of view as they approach it. One advantage with casting head-on is that a fly placed ahead of the fish will certainly be moving away from it during the retrieve. Unless the fish is greatly over-cast, there is no way to retrieve the fly toward it. If you over-cast the target zone, carefully pick up for a shorter recast if time permits, or let the fish swim by and try a perpendicular or going away shot. When presenting head-on, the fly and the fish are moving in the same direction so there is a long window of time for the fish to spot the fly and follow it, which is not the case with perpendicular casting angles. The presentation may be intended to get the attention of several fish when casting to an advancing school. This is also not the case with perpendicular casting angles.

The disadvantage to casting head-on is that the fish are closing on you and the cast must be made with enough lead to allow the fly to sink as necessary. This can make some head-on shots impossible if the fish are spotted too late. When a fish follows a fly presented head-on the angler must immediately crouch low to avoid being seen, which would quickly end the follow. The reach cast is an advanced presentation that is effective for overcoming this facet of striper fishing. Head-on also has disadvantages when fishing from a skiff since it requires a long cast to get the fly to the fish before they see the boat, angler or guide, which they can do from as far as 100 feet away in bright sun.

Perpendicular Presentations

Another common casting angle is perpendicular to the fish's track. Perpendicular presentations, or "crossing shots", are particularly effective when the fish are advancing out of the sun's glare and while fishing from a skiff. Stripers often swim by wide of a wading angler's position, making the crossing shot

CASTING HEAD-ON

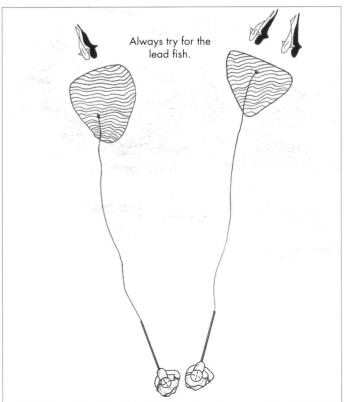

Always try for the lead fish.

THE PERPENDICULAR PRESENTATION

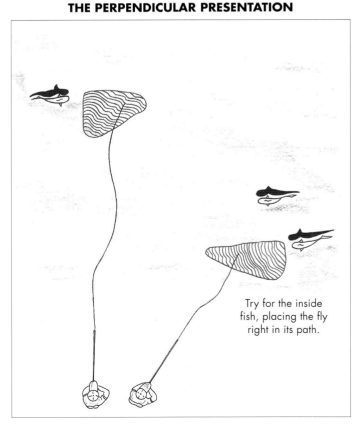

Try for the inside fish, placing the fly right in its path.

the only one possible within casting range. The same scenario prevails for anglers fishing the surf when bass are cruising well outside the wave-break.

When working offshore flats by boat, the perpendicular presentation is used to present to fish swimming wide of the skiff. Advancing fish that may be hit head-on at long range are often allowed to swim by wide so that a shorter crossing shot may be made. Now, a striper is less apt to see the boat and spook as it turns to the fly and follows briefly before striking. Very often, stripers advance down-sun as they feed (that is, swim with the sun at their backs) making them all but impossible to spot until they are abreast of the angler or skiff. Alert anglers, with an eye on the "back door", make the most of these opportunities with crossing shots.

Perpendicular presentations are carefully executed to place the fly directly in the fish's path or slightly inside by no more than four feet. It is tempting to cast well across a striper's path for a retrieve that draws the fly across the fish's nose, one that would be impossible for the fish not to see. This leads to the most common mistake while sight-fishing. Though the fly is not advancing toward the fish in this scenario, it is moving into the intercept point, not out of it, so *the distance between fish and fly is closing, not increasing.* To avoid this, position the fly inside of the fish's track, especially if the fish is at all by your position. If the fly is positioned too far inside or the retrieve started too soon, however, the fish may never see the fly. Aim for about three or four feet inside of the fish's path and start the fly moving as the fish comes to within five or ten feet of it. The retrieve is started slowly and timed so that the fly is moving off the striper's track when it is first spotted. A properly executed presentation will draw the bass off its path for a follow and subsequent strike.

When casting to multiple fish the most inside fish should be targeted with your presentation. Going for an outside fish will generally spook the ones nearest to you during the retrieve, effectively alarming all of them. See advanced presentations described below to learn how a curve cast can greatly enhance perpendicular presentations.

Drop-and-Twitch Presentations

At times stripers are reluctant to chase prey and are only interested in forage that appears right in front of them as they hunt the bottom. These fish generally move very slowly, frequently drifting nose down with the tide as they scan the bottom with "tunnel vision" for quick-burrowing prey or immobile food, such as worms. These morsels are simply inhaled off the bottom as they are encountered. The drop-and-twitch technique is ideal for taking these lazy, focused feeders. Presentations may be made at either perpendicular or head-on angles, but in either case the fly is not stripped.

The fly is placed as close to the fish's track as possible with enough lead to allow it to sink all the way to the bottom before the fish is in range of seeing it. As the fish approaches, the fly is merely twitched to entice the striper to inhale it as it swims by. The take can be very subtle and a slowly tightening line is often the only indication that the fly has been taken. Other times, the fish will roll slightly or flare its gills as it

takes. Anglers should stay alert and strip-strike (execute a quick 12-inch strip with the rod-tip down) if they observe this in order to set the hook before the fish rejects the fly. Stripers feeding in this manner can take a fly and subsequently reject it without anything being felt. Many strikes are missed because of a failure to set the hook based on a visual take.

Overhead Presentations

Striped bass are designed for overhead feeding. With eyes placed well atop the head, much like a snook's, they scan overhead for prey very well. Although most sight-fishing is done in bright light when the fish are feeding exclusively on the bottom, there are times when stripers will rise in the water column to take a fly presented overhead. Early in the sight-fishing day, from 7:30 a.m. to about 10:00 a.m., and later in the sight-fishing season when waters have cooled down are two times when bass eagerly move up in the water column to feed. Squid patterns are effective for early morning sight-fishing, while large up flies, such as Deceivers, work well late in the season as the fall migration nears.

Since the fish are swimming on or near the bottom while the fly is being presented near the surface, precise fly placement overhead is far less important than with other presentations where the fly and the fish are at the same level. A large fly is easily spotted at long distances and there is virtually no possibility of spooking fish during the retrieve. Casts may be made at any angle to the fish, but optimum fly placement is out in front. Regardless of presentation angle, the fly always moves away from the striper, which must rise in the water to capture it. These reasons combine to make overhead presentation simple and effective when the fish are willing to rise to the fly.

THE OVERHEAD PRESENTATION

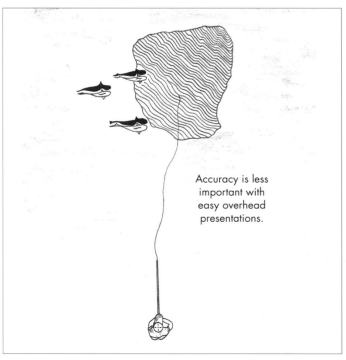

Accuracy is less important with easy overhead presentations.

Going Away Presentations

Some people call it a "Hail Mary", but when the going away presentation is executed correctly it works about half the time. Not bad odds when that's all that's left! As its name implies, this presentation is intended for stripers that have passed your position and are not looking back. Sometimes these fish are not spotted until after they have gone by you, but more often they were spotted too late to make an effective toss at them while they were advancing. Instead, savvy anglers avoid a sure spook by remaining motionless, letting these "inside and tight" fish swim by their position and then cast to them with a going away shot. This takes some discipline and patience.

The cast places the fly slightly beyond the fish by three to five feet, and to the inside (toward the angler) by two or three feet. Since you don't want to line the fish you can't lead by much more than this. Since the fish is moving away, the retrieve must be started as soon as the fly falls below the water surface. If the striper spins and follows he will almost always strike within a few strips of the fly. Accurate casting is needed here and the first shot has to be good. The fish is moving away so successive tries become progressively more difficult.

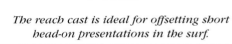

CASTING TO FISH MOVING AWAY

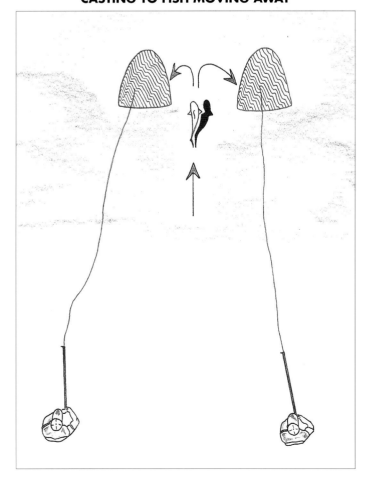

— Advanced Presentations —

The basic presentations described in the previous section will score plenty of hook-ups when properly executed. But large stripers can be very challenging at times, demanding perfect presentations and extraordinary angler stealth in order to fool them. Special casting and line-handling techniques that have been used by trout fishermen for a long time (particularly dry-fly fishermen) can help. The reach cast, curve cast and line manipulation by mending, are three advanced presentations that have relevance to saltwater sight-fishers. These age-old fly-fishing techniques are ideal for improving sight-fishing presentations and enhancing stealth on the flats.

Head-on with a Reach Cast

When presenting head-on, the reach cast is ideal for keeping a following striper off a direct path toward the angler during the retrieve. Dry-fly fishermen commonly use this technique when presenting across the current to offset the cast further upstream, enabling longer drag-free drifts. For sight-fishermen, this cast provides a simple means to offset a head-on presentation by as much as 12 or 13 feet. For long casts of 50 feet or more the reach cast is no longer effective nor is it really necessary at this range. When casting head-on at close range, however, the reach cast is excellent. Illustrations depicting reach cast presentations are presented in Chapter Seven, "Angling Strategies".

The reach cast is ideal for offsetting short head-on presentations in the surf.

Perpendicular Presentation with a Curve Cast

The curve cast is perhaps the most difficult cast to execute well with any consistency. But for those who can, it is an ideal method for keeping the retrieve of a perpendicular presentation from drawing the fly toward the fish or running an intercept course with it. Ideal fly placement with a perpendicular casting angle is directly in the fish's path, which is sometimes difficult to hit. The curve cast effectively turns a difficult perpendicular presentation of 20 to 50 feet into a head-on shot with little chance of spooking the fish *and* the retrieve draws the fish away from the angler. Curve casts become exceedingly difficult to execute consistently at longer presentation distances where they are no longer practical. Illustrations depicting curve cast presentations are presented in Chapter Seven, "Angling Strategies". For those not interested in such advanced casting, there is a far simpler method for achieving the same result—the mend, as described below.

Offsetting the Presentation with a Mend

Short crossing shots may be easily offset by making a large mend after a straight cast initially places the fly well ahead of, and slightly beyond the target fish at ranges of 20 to 40 feet. The object of this technique is the same as with a curve cast—to effectively turn a crossing shot into a head-on presentation. Though much simpler than curve casting, the mend technique is still not a mindless action. The fly must be initially placed beyond the fish's track, as it will be drawn back toward you when the big mend is made. Overshooting the target with the initial cast allows the fly to be drawn back into correct position after the mend is made. As with other presentations, the initial cast should lead the fish with enough distance to give the fly time to sink to the bottom after the mend. The start of the retrieve is timed so that the fish encounters a moving fly and moves in for the follow and strike. This technique steers an interested fish away from the angler with a retrieve that has little risk of spooking it, just as with the curve cast.

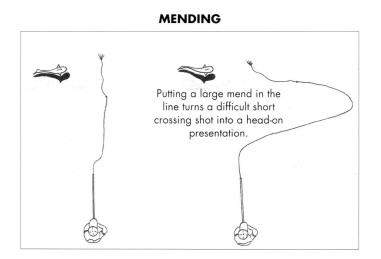

MENDING

Putting a large mend in the line turns a difficult short crossing shot into a head-on presentation.

Utilizing Currents

Except during slack tide, all sight-fishing areas have water movement. The current may be weak, as with the broad, gentle sweep of water over wide, shallow flats. Or it may strong, typical of channel flow. Currents over inshore and offshore flats most often result from tides. However, strong winds blowing over these flats for any length of time can significantly influence the prevailing water movement. Current in the surf results from many strong water movements, including waves, tides and wind. Here, the environment is dominated by dynamically changing currents that should always be figured in the presentation. Unlike the constant flow of rivers or the broad sweep of water over shallow sand flats, water movement at any point in the surf is constantly changing its speed and direction in time.

Utilizing current greatly enhances any presentation and anglers should always take a moment to assess the water movement on the flats. In some locations it may be slight and insignificant, even during peak tide flow, and may be ignored. But most often it is relevant and factoring it in the presentation will up your score.

Current is figured into the presentation by how much you lead the fish. In addition to the fish's speed and the water depth, the water's speed is accounted for by leading fish less when swimming with the current. Too long a lead here will swing the fly out of the striper's sight during the retrieve. Many times a fly can be "hung" in front of a bass for several seconds by placing it close to the fish and twitching it in slowly—the two are drifting together.

The opposite is true when fish are advancing into the current. Here, the fly should lead the fish by a wider margin, as it will be swept naturally into the bass. When timed correctly, the fly will swing across the fish's path about four feet ahead of it, appearing quite natural. Initially placing the fly too close to the fish will cause it to swing into the intercept point, appearing unnatural and spooking the fish. Ideally the fly will swing across the fish's path several feet ahead of your target, appearing as prey struggling with the current.

When stripers hold in a current to sip prey as it drifts to them, as they often do while feeding on shrimp, current becomes integral to presentation. Here, dead drifting the fly with the current is the only way to entice them. Much like dry-fly fishing, current-driven presentations have a certain window of drag-free drift, where the fly free-floats with the current and is *not swinging with it*. The reach cast extends this drag-free drift when casting cross-current, while pile or wiggle casts create several feet of drag-free drift when casting down-current.

Presenting mole crab patterns in the surf is similar. These flies must also ride with the current and not be dragged in it. Stripers do not hold in the surf, so the imitation is cast ahead of advancing fish and incoming or receding wash brings the pattern to life in front of them. Initial fly placement must account for the fish's movement and the impending water movement with enough slack built into the cast to ensure the fly rolls in front of the striper. Pile and wiggle casts work well.

Chapter 7
Angling Strategies

The goal of any sight-fishing strategy is to position the angler to intercept the most fish with the best opportunity for presentation with the fishing conditions at hand. "Fishing conditions at hand" include marine and atmospheric conditions, visibility, flat characteristics, tide conditions, water levels, size and quantity of the fish, season, forage present, and human activity on or near the flat. Because sight-fishing is affected by prevailing marine and atmospheric conditions much more than other forms of fly fishing, I've included some Internet sites in the Suggested Reading and Viewing on page 99 to help you plan and strategize your fishing. These sites provide up-to-the-minute forecast information on weather, tides, waves and water temperature. I strongly urge anglers with Internet access to utilize these and other online resources.

— Inshore Flats —

Inshore flats are best fished on foot. These waters are readily accessed from shore and the overall network of flats, channels, drop-offs and shoreline structure make wading ideal for intercepting fish in a variety of feeding situations. Because these flats are typically small and the visibility for wading anglers is inherently short, the fish are often first spotted at close range. Wading or working from the bank allows anglers to get much closer to these fish, without alerting them, to make effective short presentations.

Inshore flats may certainly be fished from a skiff and many anglers do it, but without the acres of water typical of offshore flats, and without schools of hundreds or thousands of stripers, working from a skiff is not necessary nor is it effective. Inshore flats have fewer fish cruising them and many times the same fish are seen several times throughout the day. Stealthy anglers on foot

may present to these fish multiple times (if required) without ever spooking them. Skiff anglers usually have only one shot to either hook the fish, or watch it swim to deep water for the rest of the day. In fact, the presence of a conspicuous skiff alone usually alerts the fish, often causing the entire flat to go dead in short order. Not to be confused with bonefishing or stalking stripers offshore, where many different fish are encountered while poling the shallows, inshore striper flats are fished "surgically". If a vessel is required for access, I recommend beaching or anchoring it once you're there and fishing on foot.

The nearness of the fish while making presentations leads to other considerations as well. Stealth is most important and it is achieved through a combination of visual and aural masking techniques. Anglers who pay attention to detail, dress appropriately, and move slowly and quietly will create more opportunities. Olive and gray clothing work best inshore where the surroundings are typically dark and drab as well. Move slowly when walking or wading and step softly; stripers pick up movement very well. A soft, slow gait minimizes low frequency underwater vibrations, which propagate far and fast in seawater, announcing your presence.

When fish are encountered at ranges of thirty feet or less, anglers should quickly reduce their profile by crouching low or bending forward at the waist. A low profile greatly reduces your visual image to the fish. By crouching really low you can effectively vanish from their view due to the refraction (downward bending) of the light carrying your image as it penetrates the water. Of course, you'll want to stay high enough to keep the fish in sight while making an accurate cast, but once the fly is in position and the fish shows interest, crouching to a low profile is best.

Inshore flats may be fished while wading ...

Waking fish are easily spotted in shallow water early in the morning.

Inshore flats are less sensitive to weather and may be fished under a wide range of conditions. Much less affected by the wind, and immune to surf conditions, inshore sight-fishing relies only on adequate light. A blue sky with bright sun provides ideal visibility for wading. With marginal viewing, working from the higher elevation of banks improves visibility, while posting-up creates extra time for presentation.

Stripers occasionally feed in very shallow water of 15 inches or less from first light through sunrise. The fish themselves cannot be spotted in this light, but the calm surface that generally prevails at this hour readily shows wakes and pushes as the fish work the shallows. This is very enjoyable fishing that is akin to casting to waking and tailing bonefish. Your casting lead should be lengthened to account for the fact that the fish are a few feet ahead of the push or wake that you see.

... or from the shore.

Equipment Considerations

Wading booties, or other protective footwear, are essential. Broken shells, feisty crabs and other hazards found on inshore bottoms could ruin your day if stepped on while barefoot. The coarse and sharp-tipped grasses that thrive along estuary shores are uncomfortable and hazardous as well. I highly recommend the zipper-style neoprene flats boots that are available through many outfitters. Old sneakers or moccasins simply don't compare to the boots that have been perfected specifically for this fishing.

Nine-foot rods and clear intermediate fly lines are ideal for inshore flats. Small flies, light winds and modestly-sized fish are typical here making lighter tackle preferable. Anglers may fish rods as light as a five-weight, but more often a six- or seven-weight is ideal. I fish with as light a fly line possible with the wind conditions at hand. This allows delicate presentation in slick, no-wind conditions. When the wind is up and the fish less spooky, heavier lines will cut through the wind better, making quick and accurate casts easier.

Other equipment such as chest-packs and stripping baskets may be used if anglers are more comfortable with them. I prefer to remain unencumbered and maintain mobility for wading and making presentations to fish that may appear suddenly from any direction. Crouching low is difficult with a basket and I recommend hand-carrying the shooting line in loops, as described in Chapter Six, as a better alternative. Other equipment, such as fly boxes, spare glasses, drinking water, a lunch, etc., may be conveniently carried in a canvas or waterproof gear-bag, and left ashore and out of the way. Make sure it's positioned above the tide line. Shirts with large pockets and soft fly books that may be tucked in your waistband are all the storage space you'll need for nippers, flies, small forceps, and spare tippet material. Alternate glasses may be conveniently tethered around your neck on lanyards and available for quick switches with changing light or bottom conditions.

Wading the Flats

Unless you're very tall, wading should be limited to water depths of 15 to 30 inches. With the exception of first light, stripers are rarely found in water less than a foot and a half deep. Depths above 30 inches put your eyes too close to the water's surface and make spotting very difficult. An ideal wading depth for most people is just above the knee, and plenty of stripers will be found in this water.

Initial fly selection may be based on prior experiences on the flat being fished, a guess based on prevailing habitat and time of season, or the primary prey may be read based on shore-side observation and fish behavior. Scanning the shallows for bait and the banks for remnant crab shells, or netting the bottom, as described in Chapter Three, are all effective techniques. Striper behavior reveals clues as well. Fish meandering along the bottom, stopping to focus on the bottom and tailing occasionally, are likely feeding on crabs or flounder. Stripers that cruise swiftly, rushing small pods or even individual baitfish to the top are certainly chasing sand eels or silversides. When holding deep in a current and rolling they are most likely sipping shrimp.

Anglers should initially position themselves on the flat so that productive areas are covered with the sun at their backs for optimum viewing. Stripers generally move with or against the current and your spotting will improve greatly by anticipating fish coming from these directions. They may feed in either case, however, and all fish spotted on inshore flats are good targets. Stripers frequently cruise the edges of drop-offs and sandbars, which also makes their direction of approach easy to anticipate. Wading should be slow and quiet and your entire viewing window should be scanned for advancing fish.

Unlike the tropics, where high-quality viewing prevails in all directions for several hours through mid-day, the intensity of sunlight in the north produces omni-directional viewing for a much shorter period. A reduced viewing window of 180 degrees, or less, results for most of the day and fish are frequently encountered cruising out of the sun's glare. I recommend intercepting the fish with a post-up strategy, as described later, when the main flow of fish is advancing out of the glare.

When working against the tide, a long stirred up trail of bottom sediment, known as a "mud", may be left in your wake. Stripers approaching from behind (also working into the tide), and fish that may have swum by wide of your position will investigate the mud and often follow it to its source as they sniff out food in the agitated bottom. Savvy anglers that keep a sharp eye over their shoulders are rewarded with easy shots at these hungry fish.

The majority of open-flats presentations are head-on or perpendicular, at close range in either case. To facilitate the quick, short casts often called for, I recommend using a clear fly line and a short leader about four feet in length. This allows a relatively long length of fly line (seven to ten feet) to be comfortably held out of the rod-tip while wading. The rod may now be quickly and easily loaded, enabling you to make presentations as short as 15 feet if

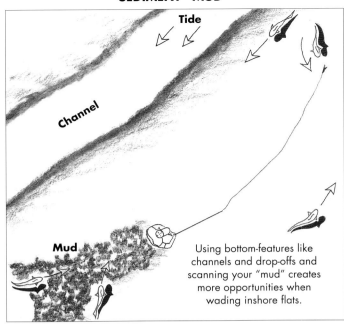

SEDIMENT "MUD"

Using bottom-features like channels and drop-offs and scanning your "mud" creates more opportunities when wading inshore flats.

needed. The short leader also allows the fly to drop down to position more quickly.

Most casts are 20 to 40 feet long and the reach cast should be used for short head-on shots. The mend technique is effective for capitalizing on short, sudden crossing shot opportunities. Fish that have gotten by you, that remain in sight and have not been alerted to your presence, may be attempted with a going away shot. If the fish appears nervous or agitated at all, you can always just let him pass and wait to spot him again later.

Working from the Banks

A higher elevation above the water provides anglers with enhanced viewing and the ability to make longer presentations when working from shoreline banks. Here, when the viewing is good, fish can be spotted well beyond casting range allowing long presentations of 40 to 70 feet to be easily made (most casts are still 30 to 50 feet). To facilitate the longer casts, I recommend leaving 10 feet of fly line out the rod-tip and standard leader lengths of eight or nine feet. The long line out of the rod is easily carried in the fingers of the line-hand while walking along the bank. Since stripers can pick up rod-flash from rods held high in bright sun, anglers should consciously carry the rod low until a cast is to be made from this higher elevation. They'll immediately change course away from the flash and quickly become lockjawed when they do.

The fish may cruise parallel to the shore some distance out during *any* phase of the tide, as long as the water is moving. Here, the added elevation increases casting range and a tall angler profile will not spook the fish at distances greater than 50 feet. Long head-on or perpendicular presentations

TYPICAL PRESENTATIONS WHEN WORKING FROM INSHORE BANKS

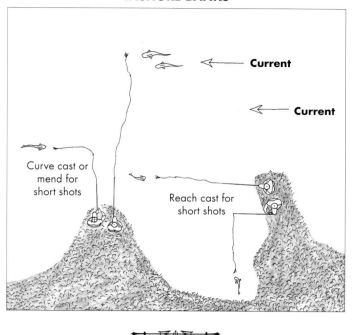

Curve cast or mend for short shots

Current

Current

Reach cast for short shots

Points are ideal for posting-up on inshore flats.

often take fish well out from the water's edge. Once a fish is following, however, anglers must still crouch as low as possible to reduce their profile against the otherwise flattened shoreline. Remember that stripers can readily pick up standing anglers from 35 feet away.

Working from the bank is very effective during high tide when the fish are poking along at the water's edge. It's best to back away from the edge several feet to keep from alerting these fish. Head-on presentations with a reach cast to fish advancing along the bank, and perpendicular casts followed-up with a mend for crossing shots are both effective for these shoreline cruisers.

A word of caution: estuary banks and other shorelines can become slippery where algae or other surface growth is present. Many times this does not become apparent until mid-day when sun and warmth somehow activate the algae, making it slippery and dangerous.

Posting-Up

Posting-up at a premium intercept point is highly recommended when the viewing is marginal during early morning or late afternoon, on hazy or bright overcast days (causing high glare), or in fog. This may be from the bank or out in the water. The fish will still be moving when you spot them and a stationary, post-up position dampens the suddenness with which the encounter takes place, allowing extra time for the presentation to be made. Because the fish are initially spotted at close range in this light, typical casting distances are reduced to 30 feet or less and a short leader is again recommended to facilitate close, quick presentations. Shore anglers may leave the shooting line in loose coils on the ground, away from their feet (much the

same as when fishing from a skiff) when in the ready position.

The short-range spotting and very narrow window of opportunity makes posting-up exciting, with fish suddenly entering your viewing window from every which direction. Approaching fish may be anticipated to some degree in certain locations, however, and knowing these directions is a distinct advantage when posted-up.

When out on the flat, drop-offs and channel edges are premium locations to post-up. When on the bank, points are ideal. Points are oftentimes flanked by shallow, fertile coves that stripers love to prowl. From a point position, an angler can scan for fish cruising by outside the point, as well as take shots at stripers working in close along the bank and in the coves. The effective range for viewing and casting from a point frequently approaches 330 degrees—an optimum situation when posted-up. Anglers often post-up when the sky is overcast. The glare-free water surface that results with a dark overcast sky generally allows spotting throughout a wide viewing window, making the point position quite advantageous.

CHART C5
Typical Casting Distance in Feet

	Striper Size Range in Pounds			
	5-10	10-20	20-30	30+
Inshore Flat	40	50	60	—
Offshore Flat	60	70	80	90
The Surf	30	40	50	60

— Offshore Flats —

Offshore sight-fishing is a team effort between angler and guide that is usually done from a skiff. By their very nature, offshore flats require a boat to gain access from the mainland. However, with good visibility and very shallow water, anglers may leave the skiff and wade with the same fishing strategies used on inshore flats. Either way, the skiff is always throttled back and the engine turned off well away from the fishing and then poled onto the flats to avoid alerting the fish and as a courtesy to others already in position.

Offshore flats are usually fished from the skiff because of the higher elevation and enhanced viewing they provide, as well as to cover more water. These flats are expansive and they often hold fish in water too deep to be effectively spotted while wading. These factors make fishing as a team from the skiff the best option to reach huge numbers of fish over large areas. Fishing from the skiff is not without drawbacks however, as the striper's keen overhead vision forces skiff-fishers to adjust their strategy in several ways in order to remain consistently successful.

The skiff itself is a blessing and a curse. Its high casting deck and poling platform provide excellent vantage for spotting, but the silhouette of the boat's hull and contents, including anglers and push-pole, are also visible to stripers. Striped bass become immediately alert and cautious in the presence of a skiff, so it becomes a game of spotting the fish and making the presentation before the fish are aware of your presence. A good team strategy will help here, but a lot of the effort rests with the angler, who must be prepared to make long casts. Here, more than with any other sight-fishing, the ability to cast long is important. Camouflaged attire is far less important now due to the relatively long casting distances and the overwhelming presence of the skiff itself. The flash from shiny objects, however, can still alert bass from long distances. Items such as fly

Successful head-on shots from the skiff call for long, accurate casts. This angler's right on target.

rods and antennas should be lowered (if possible) while fishing. This is especially true when the fish are advancing from an angle out of the sun, where reflections bounce right back in the direction of oncoming fish. Push-poles extend high in the air and dark, flat-finished poles are least visible to fish.

The sight-fishing day should commence as early as the tides (which must be figured ahead to ensure adequate water will be on the flat), the sun and your spotting ability allows. Early is good, as winds are usually as light as they will be all day and stripers are less alert with lower light levels and take a fly much more readily. Sometimes the tides call for a later start; many of the strategies discussed below are effective in bright light or high wind conditions.

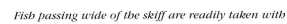

Fish passing wide of the skiff are readily taken with short crossing-shot presentations.

They're not all giants offshore, but they're all fun and exciting.

Considerable travel over open-ocean waters is usually required to get to the flats and planning around the weather is paramount to your safety. Fishing offshore flats is a boating adventure that requires some special equipment entirely unnecessary with other forms of sight-fishing. Part of your planning should involve making sure that everything will be aboard when you depart for the flats. A checklist that includes safe-boating equipment, all the necessary boat-related fishing equipment, hand-held electronics, personal gear and tackle, adequate fuel and fresh water is a wise idea.

Equipment Considerations

As far as footwear is concerned, any comfortable, non-slip, white-soled deck shoe will do. While on the casting deck, some anglers (myself included) prefer to take their shoes off and cast barefoot. By going barefoot you'll instantly know if you're stepping on your line. To those new to sight-casting, there is nothing more frustrating than blowing a prime opportunity because you were standing on your shooting line and failed to get the cast off on time. Your line and leader should be continually checked to ensure that they're not fouled on anything, as you stand ready. Keeping your shooting line clear for a presentation can be difficult on windy days, especially when the boat is rocking and you're concentrating on seeing fish. Here is where a fishing partner can be a team player. As you and your guide focus on spotting fish and making the right presentation, your partner can concentrate on your running line and keep it clear for you to cast when necessary. Knowing that you'll do the same for him or her really adds to the team spirit of this fishing. The skiff decks should be kept clear of all loose equipment while fishing to allow anglers and the guide to maneuver about the boat quickly and quietly while fishing. All rods should be stowed low (preferably under the gunwales), and antennae lowered to keep the air clear for casting in any direction.

The ready position described in Chapter Six works well for skiff fishing. The length of line you leave out the rod tip should be as long as you can comfortably handle as it enables you to load the rod quickly for long casts. With three false casts or less, the rod should be fully loaded, with 30 to 35 feet of line in the air, and ready to shoot the fly to the fish with casts of 60 to 90 feet. You must double haul your cast to achieve this distance. The double haul really builds line speed that helps power the line through the air in breezy conditions, which is important even with *short* wind casts. I don't see the need for a stripping basket when sight-casting and it often gets in the way when maneuvering to make a quick cast in an unanticipated direction. If you're more comfortable using it, then use it, but for serious sight-fishing I would practice without it.

Several factors are considered when selecting rods and lines for offshore sight-casting. First, these areas are wide-open places and the wind will be blowing more often than not; fishing in 10- to 20-knot wind is common. Second, large, wind-resistant fly patterns are often used, which can be difficult to cast into a stiff breeze. And third, offshore fish run large, with 10- to 25-pounders common targets. Nine-foot rods are easiest to handle and stow on a skiff and I recommend them over longer rods. Nine- and 10-weight rods are best, as they are powerful enough to cast large flies a long distance in the wind. Lighter rods make getting the required casts off difficult.

Most saltwater fly rods available today have very stiff, fast action and function perfectly for everyday fishing. However, loading these rods quickly and firing off long casts (starting with the fly in hand, of course) is not easy for many casters. It takes a great deal of practice to do it well. Much better sight-casting performance can be realized by overlining the rod by one line weight. For example, fishing an 11-weight line on a 10-weight rod, or a 10-weight line on a nine-weight rod. Bumping up a line size will help load the rod more quickly; only the line's head need be in the air to shoot a long cast. The greater loop energy and momentum carries large flies farther and more accurately in the wind. Line speed may be a bit slower, but this also softens presentations and spooks fewer fish.

All lines for offshore sight-casting should be weight-forward tapers in either clear intermediate or high-density, full-sink coatings. Stripers have excellent vision and they can see fly lines several feet away with bright sun and clear water. Clear intermediate lines sink below the water surface and are much less visible to wary stripers when using standard nine-foot leaders. But the striper's keen overhead vision often renders intermediate lines ineffective for offshore fishing. Here's why; long casts are often needed to get the fly to the fish before they see the skiff, which stripers do notoriously well. They also have a tendency to follow a fly for some distance before striking. A full-sinking, high-density line drops to the bottom and keeps the fly down while retrieving over a long distance far better than an intermediate line, especially when fishing from the elevated boat deck. Stripers following a fly that is rising in the water as it is retrieved toward the skiff will usually see the boat or its occupants and turn off before striking. Full-sinking lines keep the fly down much better, which keeps following stripers focused down toward the bottom rather than up toward the skiff, and they produce more hook-ups. When spotting conditions are marginal and casting distances are short, I recommend clear intermediate lines and nine-foot leaders. Bright sun and good spotting require long casts and I recommend full-sinking lines and 12-foot leaders to keep the fly down during retrieve in these conditions. Full-sink lines are preferred to heavy sink-tip lines that are difficult to cast without the line's head crashing to the water and spooking the fish.

Scientific Anglers offers clear-finished intermediate lines in tapers trade named Mastery Series Bonefish Taper and Tarpon Taper. These lines are designed for sight-casting and have compressed heads (the front taper and belly are squeezed into a shorter length at the end of the fly line) that enable rods to be loaded more quickly with less line out the tip. They are excellent for striper fishing. Several other manufacturers produce premium clear-coated lines and full-sinking lines that are fine for sight-casting as well.

Poling the Flats

When poling the flats, good communication between angler and guide is critical for quickly and accurately directing the presentation to advancing fish. The guide is in a much better position to spot fish and he or she has a sixth sense as to which presentation opportunity is best when several fish are in view. A good guide will always consider the angler's ability as well as the fishing conditions at hand when directing the cast. The direction to the target is best communicated by mentally imposing a clock face over the skiff, where twelve o'clock is toward the bow, three o'clock is to starboard, six o'clock is aft, and nine o'clock is to port. A clock heading to the fish cannot lead to confusion where "left" and "right" easily can. While setting up on the flat, some dialog as to the distance of various visible bottom features from the skiff will clarify differing impressions of distance. One man's 30 feet may be perceived as 40 feet by another, and so forth. Good communication is important.

Surveying resident prey can be difficult on offshore flats, but if possible, some read as to the prevailing forage should be made to ensure effective fly selection. Most offshore prey can be predicted somewhat based on the stage of the season; sand eels and herring in the spring; squid, sand eels and crabs in the sum-

The guide positions the skiff for an ideal presentation position.

CLOCK POSITIONING

Mentally imposing a clock face over the skiff improves communication between angler and guide.

12 o'clock

3 o'clock

9 o'clock

6 o'clock

mer; silversides and menhaden in the early fall. With a lack of any such information, I recommend starting with a large, deep-working pattern, such as a long Half & Half. Move to smaller bottom-working flies and then to up patterns until you find what works. Most guides will know which flies have been taking fish and each has favorite patterns based on past performance.

The skiff should be poled to make best use of the sun for optimum viewing. The fish will most likely be moving with or against the tide, and the skiff should be positioned to intercept these fish with good presentation opportunities. But, stripers may transit the flat in more than one direction. Alert anglers are ready for these sudden change-ups and remain prepared to cast in any direction. Both angler and guide should scan the water throughout the viewing window to capitalize on these surprises.

Poling is effective for covering large areas and many fish may be encountered when spotting conditions are good. Most times the fish and the skiff are moving in opposite directions, so only one or two casts are possible before the fish either are hooked, see the skiff, or are out of range. The fish are generally spotted while still well out of casting range giving the skiff team plenty of time to set up a good presentation. The guide may pole the skiff close to fish that otherwise would pass by out of range, or he may kick the skiff (pivot it with the pole) to better position the angler for a good shot with the wind at hand. Most fish will require no special maneuvering and will bear down head-on to the skiff. In either case, when casting head-on, longer presentations are better to get the fly to the fish before they see the skiff and veer off. The reach cast technique is of little value here since the boat itself is so large that a rod's length offset to the retrieve offers nothing. Seventy- and 80-foot casts are best when casting head-on. If longer casts can be made accurately, they should be attempted.

Most game fish, including stripers, become less alert and aware when the wind is blowing on the flats. The greater the wind velocity, the more forgiving the fish become. While a breezy day won't instantly turn a careful, cautious flats feeder into a reckless predator, it often makes them a bit more aggressive and easier to fool. The agitated water surface results in significant background noise and the fish's view up through the surface is disrupted causing an obscured, short field of view. For fly-fishers, a 10- to 15-knot breeze is an advantage that makes close encounters possible where short casts score plenty of hook-ups. Stripers may be approached to within 40 or 50 feet in windy conditions without spooking them, and head-on presentations remain effective at this range, even from a skiff.

Whatever the presentation range, anglers should always account for the relative motion of the skiff over the bottom when retrieving the fly. When moving toward the fish, the retrieve may be sped up to keep the fly moving at the desired speed. The opposite is true with the skiff moving away from the fish, where a slower retrieve or merely a twitch may be called for. The speed of the retrieve should result in a net fly movement in the water that suits the speed of the target fish and the nature of the prey being imitated.

There will be times when the fish are advancing mainly out of the sun's glare. Spotting fish in time to make presentations with this difficult situation is near impossible while poling. This special case calls for staking-out as described later, or using a special strategy called cross-poling. Here, the skiff is poled perpendicular to the viewing window rather than down-sun. Fish swimming out of the glare are cast to with perpendicular or going away presentations. The fish appear suddenly and they're moving away at a difficult angle in this situation, but quick, accurate casts score plenty of hook-ups.

Stripers passing parallel to the skiff offer excellent opportunities. Here, the fish are not on a direct path with the skiff and much shorter presentations of 40 and 50 feet will work. If the cast is made soon enough and the fly is right, the fish often pounce on it quickly and the skiff's visibility never comes into play. Even with short follows, these fish are not in a good position to see that they are being duped. The curve cast is of limited use here since crossing shots from the skiff are still longer than most people can effectively throw a curve, and straight perpendicular presentations are recommended.

Small pods of 20 fish or less, and large schools of fish swimming in wide, two-dimensional formations are routinely encountered crossing the open flats. When presenting to a school moving parallel to the skiff, the fish on the near edge

Ahhh, another ho-hum day at Monomoy.

OFFSHORE PRESENTATIONS FROM THE SKIFF

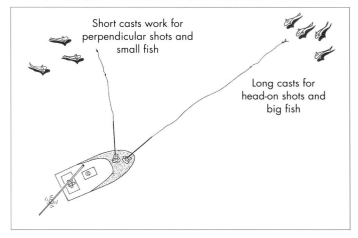

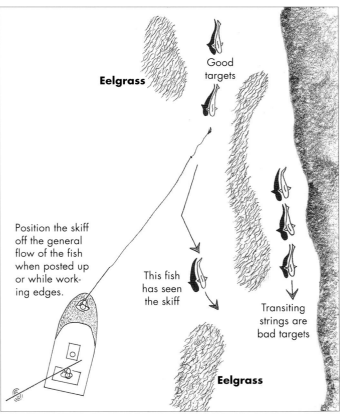

should be targeted. Several fish will still see the fly, and the retrieve will not spook any fish in the school by moving the fly towards them. When coming head-on, a fly dropped in front of the lead fish is best. Stripers schools are also found transiting along grass beds, shoals and island shorelines in elongated school formations, or progressions. Poling these edges provides excellent opportunities. The skiff should be poled against the flow of fish, which can sometimes seem endless. Many times the angler ignores the close fish and continues casting long into the flow of fish that are just coming into sight and have not yet seen the skiff. Poling these edges is very exciting fishing, often producing scores of hook-ups in a day.

Staking-Out

Marginal spotting conditions resulting from a short or narrow viewing window make staking out by securing the skiff at a strategic location your best strategy to intercept moving fish. Lack of visibility makes the motion of a poled skiff compound the suddenness with which the fish are encountered. Early morning, late afternoon, fog and dark overcast are conditions well suited to staking out.

The skiff may be secured either by anchoring on a short road from the bow or stern, or by inserting the push-pole well into the bottom at a shallow angle and tying up to it. High winds that make poling difficult or impossible are also best handled by staking-out. Anchoring has advantages in the wind. It is more secure than relying on the imbedded pole that may be loosened out of the bottom. The skiff may be held motionless by dropping anchors off the bow and the stern, which prevents the skiff from swinging. This also allows the skiff to be positioned in an orientation other than bow into the wind, if that provides a better stake-out for spotting and casting with the fishing conditions at hand. Most flats skiffs today are designed to minimize wave-slap and other hull-generated noise in order to maintain stealth. Reducing such noises should be considered when orientating the skiff as surface waves banging hard into the hull will alert fish and spoil many opportunities before they ever materialize visually.

A distinct advantage while staked-out is that the push-pole is no longer high in the air and no longer a liability for spooking the fish, thus enhancing stealth. In fact, eliminating the pole is often a good strategy even during certain bright conditions when spotting is very good. Stripers pick up the flash off equipment best when they are advancing at an angle out of the sun. The flash off the pole in this instance would be reflected right back into the eyes of the fish. Also, the fish are able to see a skiff and its contents far better and from much further away in shallow water. Therefore, when fishing water less than two feet deep, eliminating the pole from the skyline either by staking the skiff or dead-drifting with the current may be the best strategy. The success of the dead-drift

Grass edges offer ideal opportunities for offshore stake-outs.

approach of course depends on the skiff being initially positioned strategically to intercept advancing fish, while drifting at the mercy of wind and tide. The angler and guide may also consider stepping down to the skiff's cockpit deck to further reduce the visible profile. Stripers are very sensitive to movement so staking up over shallow flats is a sound strategy with any light conditions, as well.

The fish appear suddenly while staked-out, often already within casting range calling for short presentations. This is challenging, but having good reactions and a quick delivery will raise your score here. The good news is that the skiff is less visible to the fish in many instances and they are less apt to hear or see you before they see the fly. Stripers are much less aware with low light and on windy days, which allows the stake-out strategy with short casts to work. Eelgrass beds, shoals, channels and other edges are ideal places to stake the skiff as stripers frequently run these edges. On very windy days, fishing in the lee of islands may be the only option.

As an added measure of stealth, the skiff may be positioned over the bottom to take advantage of a subtle form of cover that results from underwater optics. The air-water interface behaves similarly whether viewing from above or below. That is, light is reflected from this interface downward toward the bottom just as well as upward from the top. The result is that dark bottoms cast dark reflections downward from the surface, effectively obscuring objects from above the water's surface from the view of things below the water surface. In other words, when fish pass near a dark area on the bottom, their perception of things above that water surface is temporarily degraded, much like what a white cloud above the water surface does to ours. The long and short of all this is that the skiff, under most light conditions, will be less visible if staked over a dark eelgrass bed than if over wide-open white sand. So there is hope to conceal the skiff to some degree when out in the open with seemingly nowhere to hide. This concept also holds for wading anglers who can get far closer to the fish and remain unnoticed by staying over dark or grass-bottom areas while presenting to fish transiting by over adjacent sand. The concept is most effective with a calm, glassy water surface.

— The Surf —

Sight-fishing in the surf is a unique fly-fishing experience. Here, sight-fishing strategy is unlike that of any other flats fishing. Waves and the dynamic intertidal zone surf create a challenging environment in which to fly-fish—especially when sight-fishing. The stripers found here are often large and experienced fish that would be challenging in any body of water. They are wily and not easily fooled. Ever-changing currents and waves make precise presentations a challenge that requires patience, timing, skillful casting and some understanding of the surf and its movements in order to anticipate water and fish movements to get the fly where it must be at the right time. When you've mastered sight-fishing the surf, all other sight-casting, with the possible exception of tarpon fishing, will seem comparatively easy.

When the light is good, waves provide an outstanding view. Note the second striper cruising outside the wave in the left of the picture.

Most East Coast beaches are aligned in a single, straight orientation to the sun, as opposed to crescent-shaped shorelines that receive sun from a differing direction along the beach. The general movement of fish is one-dimensional—back and forth along the shore, as opposed to the many directions possible with two-dimensional flats. This has positive and negative ramifications when sight-fishing. First, since the fish remain in the surf or otherwise close to the shore as they travel along a beach, they become available for many presentations. Once spotted, a fish may be worked for several hundred yards, as patient anglers continually reposition themselves ahead of the fish and carefully wait for the right shots. This may seem like an overly exuberant effort but many stripers found in the surf are larger than what most Northeast anglers ever hope to hook while fishing blind in other waters. Trophy fish are what make the surf exciting and well worth the extra effort. Also, other sight-fishing areas never yield such opportunity—when the fish is by you, that's it, go find another one. Here is where the surf is forgiving, take advantage of it.

Now the negative: because the fish travel one dimensionally, they will be advancing out of the sun far more often than with other flats fishing. This means that good spotting ability and accurate casting are required to make difficult perpendicular presentations to many fish that will appear out of the glare.

The superb viewing in the surf is a blessing and a curse. With good sun and sky, even a medium-sized striper can be spotted coming down the beach while still a hundred yards away through the window of a well-formed roller. Waves offer extraordinary viewing capability. The near-vertical water surface they create allows anglers to momentarily peer directly into the wave where stripers may be clearly viewed in the curl.

When locating stripers, a technique called "looking down the curl" is used to cover a lot of beach fast when the spotting is good. By following the wave toward you with your eyes as it rolls in, the entire intertidal zone may be scanned well down the beach until the wave breaks. Waves also help on days with

Surveying the surf to locate fish from a high point.

marginal viewing. The low light associated with fog or overcast is more than adequate for spotting fish in the waves, making the surf sight-fishable when other flats are not. By using high-points as lookouts, large sections of beach may be surveyed to determine the general whereabouts of fish relative to the shore, or confirm their presence at all. High dunes and jetties make ideal points from which to observe the surf from above.

As is usually the case, we rarely get something for nothing. The spotting advantage provided by incoming waves works in the fish's favor as well. Stripers also see *you* more clearly and from farther away as they peer up through the waves. This fact makes camouflaged attire and stealth more important here than on other flats. Gray, tan and sage are ideal colors as they blend well with the sand dune backdrop. Keeping your exterior free of all shiny objects is a must in the surf as well. Staying low by crouching, leaning over at the waist or squatting can remove your image from the fish's view, again due to refraction. A conscious effort should be made to reduce your profile with all head-on presentations and any time a fish is following the fly.

With good viewing, a fish may be worked for several minutes and multiple shots are possible (if required) by staying ahead of the fish as it moves in and out of the waves or straight down the beach. Typical casts are not long, nor do you want to take the long shot, unless that's all that's left. The reason is simple. The active surf can wreak havoc with long, well-made presentations, dragging them into hell and anglers into despair. When stalking a fish in the waves, timing is everything. By timing the delivery cast to fall between the arrival of incoming waves, or receding wash the angler has time to interest the fish and get it to strike before the next surge of surf ruins the retrieve. Long casts put more complex currents between the angler and the fly, making a timed approach no longer a planned or predictable technique, and the presentation is often ruined before it ever had a chance. By remaining stealthy, anglers can consistently make short, well-timed, successful presentations. I consider 45 feet a long cast in the surf.

Stripers are very alert and see very well in the surf.
Your stealth must be impeccable.

Multiple food sources make fly selection difficult in the surf.

Most are 35 feet or less. I developed the reach cast technique expressly to handle short, head-on, sight-fishing situations in the surf.

Resident prey should be surveyed to get a read as to what the fish are feeding on. Hot-zones, as revealed by clusters of crab shells, schools of bait or the accumulation of decaying seaweed (detritus), should be carefully scouted. Stationary references as to where hot-zones lie along the beach (a rock pile, a stand of trees, etc.) should be noted so that you may return to these areas or at least be alert when you're passing through them.

Striper behavior reveals clues as to what they're eating. Fish cruising slowly outside the wave-break or circling sandbars are often hunting crabs or sand eels. Stripers zigzagging quickly through the intertidal zone are most likely looking for small baitfish or shrimp. With a high tide and low surf, stripers often swim inside sandbars very close to the beach to look for worms or mole crabs rolling about the bottom. A match-the-hatch approach is required in the surf but with many prey simultaneously present, fly selection becomes difficult.

Fishing the surf is a minimalist's dream. Warm, sandy beaches are perfect conditions for barefoot wading. Occasionally, late-season sight-fishing calls for waders but that's uncommon. Going barefoot makes extensive walking and wading comfortable in the surf. It also facilitates quick maneuvering in the waves and the occasional jog needed to stay ahead of a fish moving away down the beach. Dressing light is best for the same reasons; all that are needed are shorts, a hat and a comfortable shirt. The only other absolutely necessary equipment is spare leader material, nippers and your flies, which can all be comfortably carried in shirt pockets and a soft fly book.

The surf is susceptible to adverse sight-fishing conditions resulting from large, powerful waves and a careful watch on weather and surf forecasts should be part of the overall strategy. Offshore winds associated with cold fronts usually bring fair skies, clear water and manageable surf. Outgoing tides also suppress surf to some extent and often improve the water clarity by clearing suspended sediments and by reducing the wave action, which will no longer be kicking up sand right on shore.

Equipment Considerations

Long rods of 9 1/2 feet to 10 feet are advantageous when fishing the surf. The long rod allows better manipulation of the line during complex presentations and is particularly helpful for lifting the line over small incoming waves or wash that would otherwise ruin a presentation. Long rods also permit further lateral extension during close-range reach cast presentations, helping to preserve your stealth. Any rod intended primarily for sight-fishing that isn't already matte finished should be permanently dulled, if your heart can stand to do this. I prefer to hook more fish, myself.

Clear intermediate fly lines are best. The fish don't see them well, they sink below the surface agitation (preserving the presentation), and they are easily picked up for recasting, which you may do several times while working a fish before making the perfect cast. If a heavy leader butt section is used, I recommend straightening it and dulling it before fishing. The residual coils in stiff leaders flex like a spring in the water. With bright light the fish see very well here, making light tippets or fluorocarbon leaders preferable. Light tippets also enhance the action of the fly during the retrieve, as do loop knots for attaching the fly.

Stripping baskets simplify fishing the surf by keeping the line manageable while casting and retrieving. While sight-casting, however, they interfere with the quick maneuvering that must often be done in the surf, especially in the intertidal zone. I don't recommend using a basket but I do recommend practicing casting from the ready position described in Chapter Six. This technique perfectly suits the short casts commonly made in the surf.

While I recommend fishing with as little encumbrance as possible, a variety of equipment may nonetheless be wise to have with you for a day's fishing on the beach. A variety of glasses to suit changing light conditions, fly boxes, spare leader materials, sun block, a dry, long-sleeve shirt, camera, lunch and drinking water are a few things that are always nice to have nearby when a long way out on remote beaches. These items may be conveniently carried in a canvas or weatherproof beach bag that may be safely left away from the water by the dunes.

Everything you need for a day's fishing can be conveniently carried in a canvas gear-bag.

Wading the Intertidal Zone

With reasonable viewing, the majority of fishing should be done by wading the intertidal zone in knee-deep surf. This is possible any time during the tide except high tide, where the water depth makes wading and spotting difficult from this low position and the fish are likely to be cruising the water's edge. Here, an out-of-the-water wade best, as described later. Stripers are readily spotted cruising the intertidal zone and outside the waves; sometimes from as far as 200 feet down the beach when the viewing is very good. When advancing toward you, a well-timed head-on shot is best. Anglers should reposition ahead of the fish, if possible, for a head-on presentation to fish cruising outside the wave-break. If the fish are too far out, a long crossing shot will have to do. In either case, constant repositioning ahead for casts that allow the fly to sink before the fish is in range of seeing it are desirable.

Many times fish are first spotted as they swim under surf foam or into whitewater, where they are temporarily lost from view. Patience pays here as the foam will soon clear and a close shot can be made. This is exciting and takes some nerve as the fish may reappear anywhere in front or to the side in 15 inches of water or less. If one gets by you and hasn't spooked, or you become "hand-cuffed" with a shot too close to make, than try a going away shot when the fish moves far enough off. In any case, the strong flow associated with incoming or receding wash should be figured into the presentation and retrieve. Casting well ahead of these fast-moving fish in shallow, moving water allows the fly to swing across the fish's path naturally and is most enticing.

The reach cast is ideal for close shots as it allows anglers to make short, head-on presentations to fast-moving fish. By staying ahead of fish that meander through the intertidal zone, several presentations can be made. Getting out of the water may be helpful to reposition quickly.

Fly placement is difficult with perpendicular presentations in the surf. A fly placed beyond the striper's path can easily run an intercept course with the fish during retrieve, which always spooks them. Casting too short or starting the retrieve too soon will draw the fly too far off the fish's path before it is

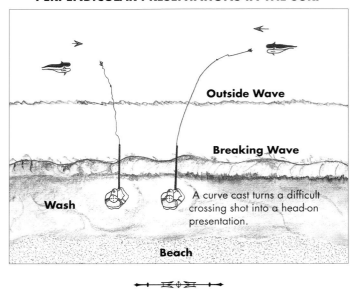

A curve cast turns a difficult crossing shot into a head-on presentation.

seen. Head-on shots avoid both of these pitfalls. Curve casts are great for fish passing perpendicular to your position at close range, which is usually the case when they advance out of the sun's glare. The curve turns a crossing shot into a head-on shot with a high probability that the fly will not approach the fish from an offensive angle.

Retrieves should suit the prey being imitated as well as the striper's behavior. Worms and mole crabs require no stripping and a drop-and-twitch approach is effective. Slow-moving cruisers outside the surf sometimes refuse to move off their course to follow the fly and a drop-and-twitch often scores with these lazy fish as well. Fast-moving fish, on the other hand, respond aggressively to briskly stripped flies. Regardless of presentation angle, it is very important to crouch low and reach whenever possible while retrieving in the intertidal zone. The shallow water and near-vertical waves allow the fish an excellent view of what's ahead of them.

At low stages of the tide with low surf and good viewing, the intertidal zone wade may be extended well out from the shoreline. Here, the same presentation principles apply, but the fish are encountered a bit differently. Outside sandbars may be readily approached to within short casting distance and stripers working these bars for crabs or shrimp may be hit head-on with ease. Deep rip tides and holes may be flanked now and fish transiting in or out of them are easily reached with short head-on or perpendicular casts. Either way, the strong currents associated with these features can be utilized to enhance presentations from this position by allowing the fly to swing into the fish's track, which is how they're expecting to intercept their prey.

Finally, from a position well out from shore, an outside-in approach may be used to scan for fish toward the beach, instead of the other way around. This is very helpful on beaches where the sun arcs across the sky over the sea, or when there is a lot of ambient glare due to haze or bright overcast. Looking shoreward greatly reduces this glare due to the dark backdrop of shoreline structure, allowing the fish to be more easily spotted.

CASTING HEAD-ON IN THE SURF

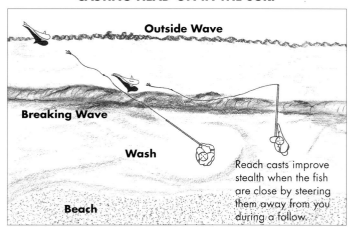

Reach casts improve stealth when the fish are close by steering them away from you during a follow.

Walking the Water's Edge and the High Beach

Stripers often cruise very near the water's edge at high tide, especially early in the day. Now, a knee-deep wade would provide a lousy view and many fish would be spooked. Instead, walking out of the water, along the water's edge, provides adequate viewing to intercept these fish with short casts. Once a fish is spotted (often at distances as short as 20 feet), repositioning further ahead and dropping a cast head-on, right along the water's edge, provides a natural presentation and a longer retrieve is possible than by casting perpendicular. Some anticipation is again required to put the fly ahead of fish advancing out of the sun, however.

Many times these early morning fish have been feeding on squid the previous night. Squid flies may be effectively fished with an overhead presentation from an out-of-the-water vantage where the higher elevation allows better spotting of vague shadows. Still, a low profile should be maintained once a fish is following. I recommend starting your sight-fishing day as early as you are able to spot fish. The fish are less critical early and simple presentations produce hookups. Everyone is different, but the earlier the better as it lengthens the day. You never know if the conditions are going to turn sour in the afternoon, which frequently happens in the summer with afternoon onshore breezes.

Walking high up the beach is known as a "high-beach wade". This is useful for spotting fish well outside the wave-break that would otherwise be very difficult to spot from a low position, especially when the spotting is hampered by glare. High-beach wades also enhance looking down the wave curl, which reveals fish still well down the beach. No presentations can be made this far from the water but anglers can easily position themselves back in the surf to intercept fish that were first spotted from the higher position.

✦—◄❖►—✦

PRESENTING FROM THE BEACH-FACE WHEN THE FISH ARE CRUISING THE WATER'S EDGE

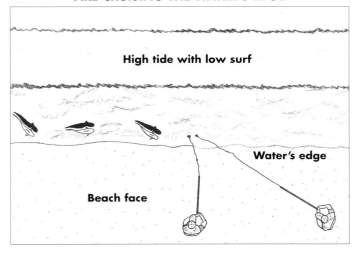

High tide with low surf

Water's edge

Beach face

High tide and low surf calls for a high-beach wade.

✦—◄❖►—✦

The Reverse Wade

As previously described, stripers frequently cruise the beach with the sun at their backs, making spotting them difficult or impossible until they are out of the sun and away from your position. They travel in one predominant direction along a beach in response to the direction of tide flow, littoral drift or wind-driven currents. Whatever the cause, there is always a slight prevailing current along the beach. Stripers often feed in the direction of this flow. There will always be some fish moving in both directions and others circling holes, but most times one direction of travel predominates.

Walking or wading into the sun while facing backwards, away from the sun, is known as a reverse wade. This technique allows anglers to cover ground and still intercept fish as they come out of the glare, swimming away. Anglers can then reposition ahead to intercept these fish as they reappear. Another way to find fish travelling down-sun is to walk very briskly with the sun at your back and overtake them as you go. Again, quickly repositioning ahead for a perpendicular shot once you find one.

Posting-Up

With marginal spotting conditions, especially fog or dark overcast skies, moving fish are encountered too suddenly while wading. Now, posting-up in a stationary position works best. Yellow lenses are ideal for spotting fish in these conditions; it's amazing how well they improve the view on a foggy day. Here, the angler selects an advantageous position and waits for the fish to swim into view. The action is generally quick as fish may swim into the viewing from either direction and they may be moving fast. Even slow-movers require good reflexes and an accurate, quick delivery. Because of the short spotting range involved, anglers usually get one shot per fish while posted-up. The fish are quickly lost from view once they're by your position and repositioning for follow-up shots is not a good option.

Hot-zones are ideal locations when posting-up since many fish can be counted on to pass through, often from a predictable direction, providing good shots. If nothing is hooked, eventually the fish will see enough flies and give the zone a rest and so should you. In fact, I immediately shift locations after taking a fish while posted-up, as the bass are too wily to continue feeding in that hot-zone.

Reading Striper Behavior

A good deal of sight-fishing involves reading the fish's behavior and adjusting your presentation accordingly. Since the sport is entirely visual, you have an opportunity to do this with every fish you encounter. While striper body language and movements can be described, there is no substitute for experience with this part of the game.

— How Stripers React to the Fly —

Any fish that veers off its course away from you before the fly is in the water has certainly seen you. But let's say that you've made the cast and the fish suddenly veers off its course, accelerating slightly, well before coming in range of seeing the fly. Most likely this fish has also seen you and is avoiding close contact. Consider these fish bad targets until they have had time to settle down. Both of these cases indicate that stealth techniques must be adjusted to suit the light, wind and water conditions at hand.

The most important element in reading the fish is interpreting its reaction to the fly. Let's say you've made your presentation and the fish is coming into range of the fly. You've started your retrieve and suddenly the fish turns off and accelerates away from the fly. Most likely the fly was running an unnatural intercept course with the advancing fish whose casual approach followed by a sudden negative reaction indicates that he didn't see you but the presentation was bad.

Now let's say you've made a good cast and the approaching fish suddenly turns, accelerates and follows the fly. You try to ignore your elevated heart rate and focus on the fish. But at the last moment it turns off. Most likely this fish also saw you, but not until it was following during the retrieve. Try to stay lower or use reach, curve or mend techniques to improve your stealth.

If you've made what you feel is a good toss at a fish, but as it swims in range of seeing the fly, you merely twitch it and he turns away sharply to avoid the fly. "What the heck happened?" This behavior is a dead giveaway that you're fishing the wrong pattern. Stripers can be funny. Like a fox that finds a rabbit in the hen house where it expects to find chicken, they sometimes get suspicious, even though rabbit is tasty. This scenario is likely to unfold whenever a single prey species predominates in an area and you're fishing the wrong imitation.

Now, you've made a good presentation and the fish shows mild interest, follows lazily and then slowly turns off as though bored and resumes hunting. You maintained your stealth! The fish liked what it first saw, the general pattern and presentation are probably OK but the fish likely didn't care for the fly's action or the retrieve. You should make an adjustment when presenting again. Most fish that take usually do so within three strips of the fly, but some will follow a long distance before striking. As long as the fish continues to follow, you're in good shape. Occasionally, speeding up the retrieve will draw a strike, but more often it causes the fish to lose interest.

When a fish has been presented a certain fly a few of times, which it followed but failed to eat, it becomes increasingly unlikely that it will change its mind and bite on successive tries. In fact, it'll become suspicious. After a couple of refusals consider that fish as needing a fresh pattern. It should still be an imitation of the same prey; the fish has told you that it's interested, you just need to try a *different fly.* Other stripers in the area may still go for the original pattern, however, so if you give up on the first fish, by all means try that fly on other fish.

Stripers rarely show zero interest in a fly. It will either be positive, as indicated by a follow, or negative as indicated by a turn off. Absolutely no response by the fish generally means that it never saw the offering—try him again. If you continue to get follows from different fish, but no strikes, you're probably fishing a fly that resembles what the fish are looking for but you need to fine-tune it to a different size or a pattern with more action or movement. When everything is right the fish accelerate to the fly and strike.

Reading the Takes

Unlike most striper feeding we're accustomed to, flats-feeders rarely take from the side. Instead, they nearly always strike from behind after brief follows. This facet of sight-fishing makes circle hooks a bad choice. The best hooks are on the small side from size six through 1/0 in O'Shaughnessy or Perfect Bend styles. Small hooks are far less conspicuous in bright light and clear water, they allow better fly action and produce more hookups. The drawback is that in very small sizes these hooks can be easily torn from a striper's mouth if too much pressure is applied. Stripers over 10 pounds can easily straighten hooks smaller than 1/0 with their jaws when hooked in the corners of the mouth.

The hook-up ...

…and the clear.

Most times, really interested fish accelerate to the fly from behind, or rise up behind it when presenting overhead, and take from behind. These fish generally hook themselves with a deliberate but nonviolent strike. Simply hold the line for a moment as it comes tight and you're on. If the strike feels tentative or you see the fish inhale the fly while lunging forward, creating slack in the line, then by all means strip-strike.

Sometimes the take is quite subtle, especially when fishing to large, lazy stripers. These fish often swim slowly, but deliberately, over the fly and inhale it as they swim by. Fish using currents, particularly in the surf, also expend very little energy during the strike and merely inhale the fly as it swings to them. In either case, any fish that rolls, sending a flash off its side, flares its gills, or writhes in a serpentine fashion when near the fly has probably eaten it. Here, a quick strip-strike is in order and you're off to the races!

Stripers are notorious head-shakers, especially the large ones. Many fish pause momentarily to violently shake their heads when first hooked. They often rise to the top in the process, giving anglers a good look at them before streaking off on their first run. Stripers can run long and fast in shallow water; similar to bonefish. Depending on their size and the strength of the tippet used, this can be as long as 175 yards with a 20-pound fish. With nowhere to go but away, even the small ones will get you deep into your backing as they run long distances back to deep water. They can really surprise you!

Releasing Your Catch

Releasing your catch is highly encouraged. With the exception of the rare instance where you've landed what you believe may be a world-record catch, or the occasional striper to be taken home and enjoyed at your family's dinner table, all stripers should be released regardless of their size. Stripers are far too valuable to sportsmen *and* to coastal economies *as a game fish* to be harvested for any other reason, including

commercial sale. The overall health of striper stocks, both today and in the years to come, depends on vigilant political efforts and a sound conscience on the part of sportsmen who pursue them for sporting pleasure.

Striped bass have many times been important in the development of this country. Sustaining early colonists in harsh times and a role in the funding the first American public schools are two examples. Thankfully, they are no longer needed in such a capacity. Today, striped bass should be excluded from commercial markets and protected and conserved as an American treasure.

Releasing your catch is simple and every conservation-minded fly-fisher knows the procedure. But for readers who are unfamiliar with it, here goes. The fish is oriented out towards open water during the release, preferably with its head in clean, well-oxygenated water. It should be held in the water with a light grip on its tail with one hand and gently supported upright with your other hand throughout the release. With its head and gills submerged, the fish is gently moved back and forth to initiate a flow of water through its gills. A gentle side-to-side motion with the tail-hand at the same time will simulate a swimming motion that engages the fish's nervous system more quickly. When the fish has regained enough "presence" to remain upright on its own and has some kick in its tail, it will swim out of your light grip on its own.

Your fly rod makes a convenient measuring device to get a read on the size of your catch. Simply hold the fish next to the rod prior to its release to get a length from its chin to the fork of its tail, which is generally referenced against the end of the rod butt. Wax pencils are terrific for putting temporary marks on rods, indicating various lengths, to facilitate quick and accurate length measurements in this way. The rod is not damaged and the wax is easily wiped off with WD-40 at the end of the season. These rod markings can easily be changed to suit different needs.

The release.

Chapter 8
Tackle and Equipment

Tackle and equipment for sight-fishing is largely the standard line-up for most Northeast saltwater fly-fishing. Some of this equipment can be modified to better meet the needs of the sight-caster and improve success on the flats. Other items, clothing in particular, are specialized in form or function and are unique to the sport. This chapter addresses specific equipment considerations for sight-fishers so that he or she can select the right tools and modify them as required to effectively stalk striped bass.

Rods

Fly-rod selection is based on three considerations: wind conditions on the flats, size of the flies to be cast, and size of the stripers you expect to cast to. Rods from 6- to 10-weight will handle virtually every combination of conditions. With small flies, small fish or light wind, I lean toward the 6- or 7-weight end of the spectrum. With large flies, large fish or a brisk wind I prefer 9- or 10-weight rods. Ideally, you'll use a rod that you can comfortably cast quickly and accurately with the weather and fishing conditions at hand.

Rod stiffness is a factor while sight-fishing. When wind and water conditions are calm, a delicate presentation greatly reduces the possibility of spooking the fish. This is also true in very shallow water of 18 inches or less. A soft rod (slow or progressive action) in these conditions opens the casting loop, allowing the fly line to drop gently on the water, thus not alarming the fish. When the wind is up this is much less of a factor and a stiff rod (fast action) is preferred to punch out the casts.

Nine-foot rods are ideal for wading inshore flats and working offshore flats by skiff. In the surf, however, a longer rod is preferred to drop short casts over wave tops, mend line in complex currents, raise the line above cresting waves or otherwise manipulate the fly line in this dynamic environment. Long rods also allow a longer reach on the retrieve; ideal with the short presentations preferred in the surf.

Fly-rod finish is a factor for sight-fishermen. Stripers, with their superb overhead vision, readily pick up flashes from above the water surface. The higher the source of flash, the further away bass may detect it. The longest, most accurate casting is possible with the rod held over-the-shoulder and a vertical stroke. This makes gloss-finished rods a liability on the flats. Many fish that seem hopelessly lockjawed or move quickly away from an otherwise well-presented fly have already been spooked by rod-flash. To avoid this and maintain my stealth, I prefer rods with matte finishes that reflect less light. Some manufacturers sell rods already in this condition (G. Loomis and Cape Fear, for example), but unfortunately many do not. To remedy this situation I thoroughly remove the gloss finish from my sight-fishing rods with a Scotch Pad. While it may sting a bit to scuff the shine from a beautifully crafted rod, doing so will improve the rod's fishing performance and boost your scorecard on the flats.

Reels

Any good saltwater fly reel that has a smooth, quality drag and holds 150 to 200 yards of 20-pound-test Dacron backing will

Many reel manufacturers produce all-black reels, including Billy Pate and Tibor reels, Ross Reels and Scientific Anglers.

get the job done. The emphasis today on wide arbor reels is less of a factor in striper fishing than with other high-velocity species. However, the preservation of a large working-spool diameter is an advantage when pursuing big, long-running stripers with light tippets. With nowhere to go on shallow flats but away, most bass will run a long distance when played with a light drag. A wide arbor maintains a large working-spool diameter, keeping the spool from spinning quickly, and preserving a sensitive drag when your backing is low.

Reels with a minimum of shine are preferred, again, to help maintain your stealth. I don't recommend dulling the finish on reels, but there are several on the market to pick from that come in all-black finishes such as Billy Pate and Tibor reels. Others, such as Scientific Anglers and Ross Reels not only come in all black, but they are matte-finished as well.

Lines

All lines for sight-fishing should have a weight-forward taper—the standard for saltwater fishing. These lines should be maintained in good condition and the running- or shooting-line portions kept clean and slick to make the long, quick casts that are often needed to get to the fish before they're too close. Running lines should be cleaned often and old, worn lines that no longer fly through the guides should be discarded.

While floating lines are the choice for bonefish, tarpon, and permit, they are out of place on the striper flats. Once again, the striper's keen overhead vision comes into play. Floating lines are opaque and, generally, brightly colored to help anglers see where their leader and fly are after the cast and during retrieve. They are also visible to stripers in clear, shallow water. The bottom shadows and surface disturbances they create are also readily picked up by bass, which become alarmed when they see them.

Floating lines also tend to bring the fly up in the water column during the retrieve; another bad feature. Stripers can follow a long way before striking and the fly's rise toward the

surface is not only unnatural for most bottom-prey, it directs the fish's visual focus upward and in the angler's direction. Stripers like cool waters. Flies presented at the fish's level, and kept there throughout the retrieve, allow fish to inspect them before striking without moving upward into warm surface water, which they are reluctant to do. For these reasons, all fly lines for sight-fishing should be either intermediate or fast full-sinking densities.

The best line for most striper fishing on the flats is the clear intermediate. The sink rate is perfect when wading flats or surf fishing with three feet of water or less. Fast-sinking lines are the best choice when fishing deeper flats, and they are preferable when fishing from a skiff. The long casts common to skiff-fishing, coupled with a higher angler elevation above the water, cause intermediate lines to draw the fly up during the retrieve. This phenomenon often causes stripers to lose interest after a brief follow because they either see the skiff or they are reluctant to rise above a certain level in the water column.

The smooth, transition-free taper of full-sink lines makes them easy to cast quickly at any range, and they land delicately upon the water. Sink-tip and intermediate wet-tip lines are tempting choices, however, they are difficult to cast smoothly and quietly. The hard landings that often result with these lines, especially on long casts, easily spook stripers with calm conditions, which makes them undesirable for day-in and day-out sight-fishing. If I were to own a single line for sight-fishing it would be the clear intermediate, full-sink line. Several premium fly-line manufacturers offer this very popular saltwater line. Scientific Anglers' clear-finish lines are great for warmwater conditions and the stiff, braided line core shoots nicely. Limp monocore lines stay coil-free and cast better in cool conditions sometimes encountered while sight-fishing.

Clear fly-line finishes are great for keeping the line out of sight from alert, flats-feeding stripers. Because of their relative invisibility, shorter leaders may be used, which in turn create much better depth control of the fly. When these lines are new, they usually have a shiny, slick finish throughout their length, regardless of manufacturer. This shine may alert stripers, but it may be easily suppressed without damaging the line's coating by lightly rubbing the entire head with a Scotch Pad. This treatment does not impair casting since the head of the line will most likely be out of the rod tip before shooting the cast, and the slick running line will still run out through the guides easily. Just a light rub with a Scotch Pad is all that is required to kill the line head's shine to fool more fish in bright light conditions. Stripers can pick up flash from this shiny finish in the air, while the line is being false cast, as well as during the retrieve when the line is submerged.

To better handle the casting challenges while sight-fishing, two line adjustments should considered. First, utilizing a line weight one size heavier than the rod being fished will help load the rod more quickly, allowing anglers to make faster presentations with fewer false casts. The heavier line also delivers the cast more smoothly with less line speed, which can soften the presentation and improve stealth in calm conditions. Second, cutting the last five to eight feet off the end of a fly line beefs up the end of the line where the leader attaches by removing the narrowest part of the taper. The line's head is somewhat compressed now, with more weight in a shorter length at the end of the line. This modification also improves how easily the line may load the rod, especially in windy conditions. A shorter line out the rod-tip will still load the rod, but it's easier to handle in the wind. The compressed head compromises the line's ability to land softly, but it cuts through the air more effectively and turn leaders over better in very windy conditions, where delicate presentations are much less of a factor. This is especially true when casting into the wind. An extreme modification would completely remove the end taper, much like the specialized "wind lines" on the market today.

Leaders

Sight-fishing leaders require special consideration.

Leader length:

When fishing clear intermediate fly lines, I recommend a minimum leader length of eight or nine feet. In bright light, stripers can still see a clear fly line if it's too close to the fly and leaders under eight feet long should be avoided. With opaque fly lines, whether intermediate or fast-sinking, I recommend lengthening the leader to 12 or 13 feet to distance the fly well away from the line. You'll know that a leader's too short if stripers follow briefly and turn off, or they over-run the fly and swim up the line to see what's at the other end.

Leader Size and Color:

Sight-fishing leaders should preferably be clear. A faint blue, gray or pink tint is acceptable but darker tints, such as the browns and greens commonly used in fresh water, should be avoided. A good test here is that if a leader material is readily visible to *you* in the water, then it will certainly be too conspicuous for stripers in bright conditions.

I typically fish with tippets of 10-pound test or less and I don't fish with fluorocarbon leader material. I have not experienced problems with fish shying from tippets of this size and I don't think that fluorocarbon is relevant when fishing tippets this light. However, fishing one day with John Prigmore on the Monomoy flats convinced me otherwise with regard to heavier tippets. While I was using a six-pound-test tippet and hooking-up regularly, John was fishing 16-pound test and was not. After he had made several quality presentations without takes, our guide examined John's leader and quickly replaced the tippet with 12-pound-test fluorocarbon. He immediately started to get strikes and we each hooked-up about as frequently for the remainder of the day. Needless to say, we were both convinced of fluorocarbon's effectiveness with heavy tippets while sight-fishing.

I recommend fishing light tippets in the six- to 12-pound-test category for three reasons. First, as described above, light tippets are less offensive to the fish (especially the larger ones) and will draw more strikes. Second, far better fly action is possible with light tippets, which also draws more strikes. In order for a striper to take, the fly must appear *and move* quite

naturally. Light tippets improve a fly's action considerably, especially weighted patterns that "hop" along the bottom like the Clouser Minnow. Third, there are no obstructions or hazards to contend with on clear, shallow sand-flats and the fish will want to energetically run long distances when hooked. There's nothing to gain by putting heat on these fish except to dampen the thrill and excitement of this sport so light tippets present no real liability.

Leader Construction:

I believe in keeping leaders as simple as possible for a number of reasons. Simply constructed leaders are quicker and easier to tie and you'll be more apt to replace them before it's too late. Fewer knots in a leader section mean fewer possible weak spots due to a worn or otherwise bad knot. Knots can also pick up debris in the water (seaweed, etc.) which can ruin the entire appearance of your presentation—again, the fewer knots the better. With today's stiff, powerful saltwater rods, scientifically concocted tapers are unnecessary to turn over eight- and 10-foot leaders. For these reasons, I recommend using a straight piece of monofilament for 12-pound-test leaders and above. For lighter tippets, a 15- or 20-pound-test butt section 2/3 the length of the entire leader may be used. The butt may then be attached to the remaining 1/3 tippet section with a loop-to-loop connection. I like the loop-to-loop attachment as it avoids the need for the difficult knots required when attaching monofilament of widely differing diameters, and it facilitates quick and easy tippet replacement. Knotless, tapered leaders are of course a simple, albeit expensive, option.

As a final note on leader construction, I remove the shine from a heavy butt section of a new leader with a Scotch Pad when I suspect that wizened fish are spooking from a shiny monofilament finish. The spring-like coils that form in memory-prone monofilament should always be removed by stretching the leader before use. This will enhance the precision of your presentation and eliminate the flash caused by these butt section coils "flexing" during the retrieve.

Stretching lines and leaders before each day of sight-fishing should become a habit.

You can dress him up, but you can't take this guy anywhere near the fish.

Knots and Rigging

To facilitate quick fly-line changes, I attach the fly line to the backing with a loop-to-loop connection. The best loop knot for the Dacron backing is the Bimini twist, but simpler knots will work fine. At the end of each of my fly lines I splice a small permanent loop. I secure this loop with a series of short, epoxy-coated nail knots—two or three are sufficient.

To facilitate quick and easy leader changes, I attach the leader butt to the end of the fly line with a loop-to-loop connection as well. Here, I permanently attach a short piece of 20- or 30-pound-test monofilament to the end of the fly line with an epoxy-coated nail knot. Either a surgeon's loop or a perfection loop is then made in this monofilament, which completes the permanent loop construction at the end of the fly line. The entire loop is about three to five inches long. I also use either a surgeon's loop or perfection loop in the leader butt, which may then be easily connected to the fly line with a loop-to-loop connection.

When using two-part leaders, I again favor the loop-to-loop connection of the leader tippet to the leader butt for simplicity. The Surgeon's Loop or the Perfection Loop are also great for this connection.

Flies may be attached to the leader tippet with whichever knot(s) you're comfortable. When using a direct knot, I prefer the improved clinch. It's easy to tie and it holds well. When using a loop knot, I prefer the Homer Rhode loop knot, but remember it tests out at about 60 percent of the strength of the material it's tied in. This knot is easy to tie and it will not slip tight when under strain, as other loop knots will. A loop knot is highly recommended to improve the action of bottom working Clouser Minnow-type flies.

The details of tying all of these knots are available in numerous fishing texts, some of which are solely devoted to knots and rigging. I strongly urge all fly fishermen to purchase one of these books, if you don't already own one.

Now there's a well-dressed sight-fisher.

Clothing and Footwear

To preserve your stealth while stalking stripers it is imperative to wear clothing that not only protects you from the sun but also camouflages you from the fish. I recommend drab or dull clothing to help conceal you on the flats. Bright colors, especially whites and yellows, should be avoided. Stripers readily pick up anglers wearing bright, conspicuous colors—sometimes long before anglers see them. When fishing inshore flats I suggest gray, green or olive attire. On bright beaches, sage, tan and khaki work best. These considerations are far less important when fishing from a skiff since the angler is much further from his quarry and the skiff itself is such a significant and overwhelming presence that personal angler stealth becomes irrelevant.

Light rays refract, or bend, as they penetrate the water's surface, and the further objects are above the water's surface the better the fish see them as a result. With this fact in mind it is clear that the further up your body profile you go the more important it is to wear something dull. For this reason I stress that hats and shirts be drab-colored. The point is that the right shorts and a perfectly colored fly fishing shirt can be all for naught simply because you chose to wear a white hat!

In general, avoid wearing any shiny objects while stalking the flats. Lots of metallic gadgets and gizmos, such as hook-removal forceps, pliers, etc. that are commonly dangled in front by fly-fishers for easy access should be avoided. Experienced bonefishers know this and several outfitters now offer these items in matte-black finishes. I even roll my watch to the inside of my wrist whenever stalking stripers on foot. By fishing "light", keeping only the items you can't do without concealed in a pocket or a pack, you'll have gone a long way in maintaining your stealth.

Sun exposure is intensified on the flats due to reflection of the sun's rays off the water. This effect nearly doubles what would be experienced on dry land. I therefore recommend long-sleeve shirts and the liberal use of sun block with a SPF rating of at least 15 on all exposed skin. Those with especially fair skin might also consider Sun Gloves for added protection on the tops of hands.

Two options are available regarding footwear for skiff fishing. White-soled, non-skid deck shoes (preferably without laces that can foul with loose or wind-blown fly line) or going barefoot. These shoes provide safe footing while aboard a bouncing boat and they won't mark the decks (a pet peeve of most flats guides). Going barefoot allows you to instantly know if you're standing on your fly line and is always my choice on calm days with dry decks—don't forget the sun block!

When wading inshore flats I recommend wearing any of the neoprene flats booties that have been specifically developed for flats fishing. The need for foot protection while fishing from marshes and over shell-strewn bottoms is imperative. Zippered flats-booties are available from L.L.Bean, StreamLine and Cabela's.

Going barefoot is your best option in the surf where ocean waters are generally warm and the fine-sand bottoms are hazard-free. It's also a very pleasurable way to fish. As waters cool late in the sight-fishing season a pair of light waders may be worn to stay comfortably dry. The color of these boots should be tan, sage or olive to again maintain your stealth.

The Flats Skiff

While a variety of watercraft may be employed to stalk the flats (provided they have a shallow enough draft), an entire class of fishing craft, known as the flats skiff, has been developed expressly for this type of fishing. These unique craft have special features that tailor them to shallow-water fly-fishing and they are ideal for striped bass sight-fishing.

A quality flats skiff is a stealthy vessel. A very shallow draft allows them to enter shallow water where stripers are stalked, and to be staked or maneuvered with silent poling over these waters. Their hulls are designed for speed to cover more water and get you to the fish fast; and they are also quiet. A well-designed skiff has a low-freeboard that keeps the angler low to the water and minimizes errant hull noise due to wave-slap that would betray the vessel's presence long before the fish are in casting range. A low profile and a hull

Wading boots are a must on inshore flats.

A poling platform – every well-equipped flats skiff has one.

Trailers provide mobility. Many guides expand their range this way to pursue more angling opportunities.

color that compliments the surroundings (pale blues and greens are ideal) go a long way in camouflaging the skiff, as much as one can be concealed on the open flats. The shallow draft and low freeboard also make them less wind and water resistant and much easier to pole over windswept flats.

Most flats skiffs are fitted with a poling platform over the engine well. From this raised position a guide can more effectively maneuver the skiff with the pole to cover the flat and position the angler for ideal presentations in the wind. The guide can also see the fish and the presentation better from this higher elevation, allowing him or her to effectively coach the angler. Push-poles are made of composite materials making them strong and lightweight. Poling a skiff, especially in deep water, is a skill that takes time to master. If you fish with a guide, odds are he or she will make it seem easy. It is not—it is hard work! The pole may also be use to stake the skiff when posting-up on a prime position, which is often done in lieu of anchoring.

Push-poles generally come in black or white. I recommend a black pole for stalking stripers as it reflects less light. As with rods, the pole becomes stealthy when it is matte-finished; a Scotch Pad works here as well. When not needed, while posted-up or on a comfortable drift with the wind, the pole should be stowed down in its deck cleats or otherwise

carried low to prevent it from alerting fish in the same manner that a rod or antennae can. The very long poles common for tarpon fishing may not be the best choice when stalking stripers, which is always done in relatively shallow water. Perhaps a short pole will become the standard for striper fishing as the sport evolves in time (make it flat gray too).

The topsides of the skiff are neat, flat and entirely uncluttered. This layout facilitates easy maneuvering about the decks and prevents loose fly line from fouling when casting to fish (this is really important when the wind is up). Anglers stand on the open bow deck, which serves as the casting platform from which they can present the fly in any direction. Many skiffs are equipped with neat, under-the-gunwale rod storage, which keeps rods not in use out of your backcast and away from your shooting line. Today's carry-on electronics also augment the clean, open topside of the flats skiff by eliminating the need for high-standing antennae that would destroy the entire concept. Radio and positioning electronics are portable and may be stowed in waterproof boat bags.

An important feature for any skiff is that it is trailerable. The mobility offered by trailering expands available fishing range by hundreds of miles. Most of today's top guides stay mobile to provide their clients the best possible fishing throughout the season.

Chapter 9
Sight-Fishing Destinations

Northeast sight-fishing opportunities are abundant from New Jersey to southern Maine on flats of every type and size found along the coast. Certain factors combine to make the Northeast *the* destination to sight-fish for stripers. Mainly, annual striped bass migrations bring the fish to these shores during the recognized sight-fishing season of May through September. Secondly, cool Northeast waters remain consistently clear through the summer, and they support robust food supplies for stripers, especially on the flats. Poor water clarity is often a problem in the mid-Atlantic region to the south, and the dearth of quality sand flats along the deep, rocky shores of Maine and Canada to the north largely exclude these portions of the striper's Atlantic range from the sight-fishing picture.

Certain Northeast destinations are blessed with premium waters and they offer outstanding opportunities. The flats associated with these areas are so perfect for sight-casting and consistently productive that some have become synonymous with sight-fishing itself. Most notable are the Monomoy flats off Cape Cod and the Norwalk Islands. The flats associated with most of these destinations are also large, often measured in square miles, or in miles of quality beach.

The Norwalk Islands, Gardiners Bay, Long Island, the southern New England coast, Martha's Vineyard, Nantucket, the Monomoy Islands, and Cape Cod Bay offer exceptional sight-fishing. These fisheries are characterized by men who know them well, as they generously share their knowledge and insight in the essays that follow. Other notable areas include Cape Cod's Pleasant Bay, Boston's North Shore, Plum Island, Massachusetts and the network of bays and barrier beaches that form the south shore of Long Island. Future striped bass sight-fisheries will surely discovered, and they may well be on the West Coast in the San Francisco Bay delta region.

The Norwalk Islands, Connecticut
(Captain Jeff Northrop)

The Norwalk Islands, considered by many as the birthplace of Northeast saltwater fly-fishing consists of 32 islands and hammocks located off Westport and Norwalk, Connecticut. It was in these very islands that Hemingway and Lerner set early fly-rod striper records. This history was to continue throughout the years with records by Capt. Pete Kriewalds and later by John Baldino in 1980 with a 71-pound striper taken with conventional tackle in Middle Passage.

The reason the islands have produced so many record fish over the years is directly tied to their location on the migratory path of the Hudson River stripers. These vast herds of fish leave the Hudson in late April and May, and journey northward in search of abundant food sources. The Norwalk Islands, located 52 miles from the mouth of the Hudson and directly at the mouth of seven rivers and streams, provides a virtual supermarket for these migrating fish. Abundant forage consists of shiners in the spring, sand eels in May and June, calico crab (lady crab) and cinder worm hatches in July and August, topped off in the fall with peanut bunker, anchovies, more crabs, molting lobsters,

The flats skiff made its Northern debut in the Norwalk Islands.

Bozo Hair Bunker and it is tied with a synthetic fiber used for clown wigs. This fiber gives a wide profile but can be cast on rods as light as a 6-weight. The rod that is most favored for flats fishing in the Norwalk Islands is the 9-foot 7-weight loaded with a 250-grain Teeny for moving water, and a 9-foot 9-weight with a 9-weight floating or intermediate for the skinny stuff. Remember, when fishing the flats it is critical to have a reel with sufficient backing and a smooth drag. Unlike deep water where the fish sounds when hooked, the flats-hooked fish has nowhere to go but away or straight up in the air. I hooked a bluefish one day while fishing the Land of the Giants that tail-walked like a tarpon and ran out 150-plus yards of backing on its first run!

I have spent 33 years fly fishing in salt water, and have been fortunate enough to have fished all over the world, but nowhere have I found a flats fishery that is this consistent and this unspoiled anywhere in the Northeast.

Sight-fishing in the Norwalk Islands.

shrimp and squid. No wonder this area holds bass all season long.

We start our year in April fishing the mud flats around Cedar Hammock using small olive and white Deceivers and Clouser Minnows. This area is a mud flat with several rock piles located at the mouth of Village Creek and Wilson's Cove, accessible only by boat. Remember, in the spring it's these dark bottom areas that warm up first and hold fish. As the season progresses the sand eels hatch on the sandy flats along the shoreline. Sherwood Island State Park and Old Mill Beach, both located at the out falls of the Sherwood Millpond, produce consistent fishing throughout the year but really light up during the sand eel and cinder worm hatches.

The mean depth throughout the island chain is approximately six feet, but please take into account that the average tide is around 6.5 feet. This tidal range produces a legendary flats fishery but makes it extremely dangerous for the novice boat operator. It was for this very reason that I brought the first flats boats to New England in the early 1980s. These skiffs, 17 to 20 feet in size, draw only 6" to 11" of water' allowing the angler to maneuver in and around the treacherous rock piles and flats that make up this area. I find fishing the falling tide to be the most productive cycle of the tide. This is when the schools of bait get flushed out of the rivers and onto the flats. Calf Pasture Flat, located off Calf Pasture Island and at the mouth of the Norwalk River, is one of my favorite flats. Referred to by local skiff guides as the "Land of the Giants", this flat has produced dozens of record-sized bluefish. When these mega-blues show up on this flat to spawn, they actually daisy chain like tarpon and can be seen tailing like bonefish. This is a true sight-fishery where stealth and accuracy are paramount.

The flats and rips around Cockeno Island are killer fall spots, producing many of my grand slams. By the middle of October through November the Islands produce a non-stop blitz. One day during 1998 we had blitzing stripers stretching from Cockeno westward to Sheffield Island. The fall fly of choice in our area is a fly I created in 1989 called the

Gardiners Bay, Long Island, New York
(Captain Paul Dixon)

In 1634, a young English officer and engineer by the name of Lion Gardiner was commissioned by Lord Say and Lord Brook of the English admiralty to sail across the Atlantic and build a fort at the mouth of the Connecticut River. After a long, exhausting journey, Gardiner landed at what is now known as Saybrook and stated, "I would rather fight every Indian in the New World than cross that terrible sea again." Oh, how those words would ring true. After building his fort, Gardiner and his band of men were besieged by the Pequot Indians for the next four years. Fighting the Pequots would later prove beneficial to Gardiner in his dealings with the Montauk Indians, arch enemies of the Pequots.

Upon completion of his commission, Gardiner sailed across to Long Island searching for a place for him and his wife, Mary, to settle. Visiting various islands off the East End of Long Island, Gardiner chose the island that the Montauk Indians called Manchonat. The abundance of game and fresh water made the island highly desirable. Trading the Indian chief of Long Island, Yovowan, ten coats of trading cloth and acquiring a land grant from Charles I to make it official, Gardiner called his new island Isle of Wight because the shape reminded him of the Isle of Wight back home in England.

Now called Gardiners Island, it has remained in the Gardiner family for 350 years. Approximately 3500 acres with 27 miles of shoreline, it is the largest privately held island in the country. Never developed, Gardiners Island has remained much the same as it was when the Wyandance, Chief of the Montauks, and his tribe speared striped bass in the clear shallows surrounding the island. Currently, the mythical weapon of choice is the fly rod for stalking the wily striper, and Gardiners Bay is certainly the happy hunting ground.

Sticking out in the cobalt blue Atlantic Ocean, the island is washed daily with fresh, clean, see-through water. The bay's crystalline water combined with its diversity of flats, shoals, estuaries and beaches makes sight-fishing for stripers here truly world class.

Gardiner's Island has a rich and colorful history.

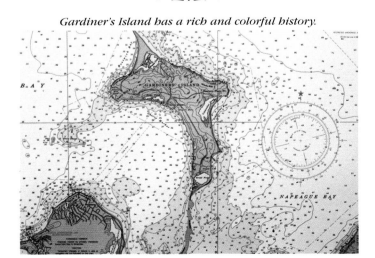

Long Island is shaped like a hundred-mile-long king crab's claw, with Gardiners Island caught in between its two pinchers. At the top of the pinchers is Plum Island on the North Shore. Plum Island is the forbidden island of Dr. Moroeu. Like Moroeu's island of weird animal experimentation, this island is the US government's super-secret research center for biological and animal testing. Maybe this is why Plum Gut is known for its monster stripers. Plum Island lies on the northern border of Gardiners Bay.

Gardiners Bay encompasses an expansive area. Like the Florida Keys, it is not unusual to run 20 minutes to the next flat to catch the tide. What makes the bay bountiful is not the size of the area but the estuaries that lie within the bay. Rich nurseries filled with baitfish, crabs and shrimp—a liquid cafeteria for the stripers and blues.

Hallock Bay on the North Shore, Coecles Harbor on Shelter Island, Napeaque, Acabonack and Three Mile Harbor in East Hampton are all estuaries that provide the ingredients for the bay's sea life bouillabaisse. Gardiners Island itself has two salt ponds that pour forth the cornucopia of creatures for which the stripers prowl the shallows.

The season for sight-fishing in the bay can begin as early as mid-April, especially if there has been a mild winter season. Mid-winter catches of stripers in dragger's nets off of Gardiners and Long Island Sound indicate that not all the bass depart to the Chesapeake and Hudson river systems. Many smaller fish seem to hunker down for the winter in deeper waters surrounding Long Island. In May, the fish begin arriving en masse. Not only the bass, famished after a long arduous winter in their natal river but also found are the sand eels and spearing that make up their early-season diet.

By June the big bass start showing, along with "toads" (very large striped bass) that make your heart race and your knees shake when spotted meandering down the flat. There are huge dream fish that travel in singles or doubles. Their peers probably caught and eaten years ago. Gardiners Bay is humming with life in June. All the links in the food chain are colliding. The sand eels are thick on the beaches, wriggling black clouds, drifting to-and-fro with the tide. The spearing are in the shoreline grasses, future french-fries for ravenous stripers.

At night in June, cinder worm swarms happen around the full and new moon phases. Not important to daytime fishing, the worm-swarms are indicators of coincident daylight crab hatches. Millions of tiny crabs, the size of the nail on your pinkie finger, hatch and flow out of the estuaries on the outgoing tides. The bass act like trout sipping the tiny crustaceans during the day. It is very frustrating to fish the crab hatch due to the very small size of the creature but it provides challenging and very visual sport. This is all part of the fabulous sight-fishing in Gardeners Bay.

The area is best fished from a boat. There is wade fishing, but beach access and parking is by permit only. This is the Hamptons and access is not easy. Poling a boat is one of the most effective methods for stalking the easily spooked striper. Very similar to bonefishing in the Florida Keys, poling is a team effort, requiring synchronization between the guide and caster. Once the fish is spotted the boat is put in position to set up the cast, providing the angler with the best shot. If all

A fine Long Island striper.

goes well you'll watch Mr. Toad track and inhale your fly, only feet from the boat. It's enough to send shivers down any fly-rodder's spine.

Some flats in Gardiners Bay may look like the white, pristine Bahamas. Many are just beaches, shoreline and shoals that may have up to six feet of water covering them at high tide. As the tide ebbs, they become hunting grounds for striped bass. Many flats inside the estuaries, like Hallock Bay or Coecles Harbor may have only two feet of water at high tide. It is best fished at the top of the tide. While outside of the estuaries the water may be six feet, fishing mid-tide to the last of the ebb usually provides the best results. Cartwright, one of the best-known sight-fishing shoals on the island, can be fished at all phases of the tide. It is just a matter of figuring when the stripers, and often bluefish, will be there feeding and cruising.

The modern-day weapon of choice for sight-fishing Gardiners is an 8- or 9-weight fly rod equipped with an intermediate line. The stripers are easily frightened so a delicate presentation is often necessary. An intermediate line keeps the fly tracking deeper, longer. If the fish comes up chasing the fly in the water column they often see the angler and guide and spook.

Getting the fly down to the striper's level is important, especially on deeper flats. Clousers, Half-and-Halfs or any weighted flies that match the bait seem to work best. Sometimes it is even necessary to utilize a sinking-head to fish the deeper edges that have stronger currents. Occasionally the stripers in Gardiners will tail just like bonefish. This is when a delicate presentation with lightly weighted or unweighted flies may be the key to success.

Oftentimes in August the fish may get finicky. Whether due to the overabundance of available bait in the bay, or warmer waters and the striper's lower metabolism, these late-summer fish can be tough to feed. This is when throwing crab patterns like Merkins, Ragheads or Rattle Crabs can be just the ticket. Lobster and shrimp patterns often fool these lock-jawed stripers.

When sight-fishing around Gardiners Island you can't help but appreciate the untouched natural beauty. Osprey circle overhead hunting for a meal in the crystal-clear waters.

Black back gulls raising their young, squawking incessantly, sending warnings to stay clear of their private island as you pole down Cartwright shoal. Also visible are wolf packs of blues, cruising the shore slamming pods of baitfish swimming for their lives. Cliffs, long eroded by the constant pummeling of the winter nor'easters, crumbling into the bay creating beautiful cream flats, perfect for seeing the striped ones coming at you two hundred feet away. Gardiners is an island steeped in history and filled with adventure for the fly-rodder.

In June of 1699, Captain William Kidd, the famous pirate, landed on Gardiners Island and buried his treasure of gold and jewels. He warned John Gardiner, grandson of Lion Gardiner, that if his treasure was missing upon his return, he would cut off the head of him and his sons. Kidd was later captured and hung in London. The treasure was recovered by the Gardiners and sent to the King of England. Occasionally, people still try and sneak on the island and hunt for the gold and jewels, but the real treasures of Gardiners Island are the stripers and blues that roam the clear waters of Gardiners Bay. The true treasure-seekers of today are hunting for striped jewels by waving nine-foot graphite rods. Not much has changed on Gardiners since the time when Wyandance and his people speared stripers in the shallows, only the weapon of the hunt.

Southern New England
(Alan Caolo)

Rhode Island and southeastern Connecticut offer unique sight-fishing opportunities. While these coastlines lack the dramatic off-shore sand flats associated with Monomoy and Nantucket, they are rich with inshore flats and are home to some of the most spectacular sight-fishing beaches in the sport. There are some off-shore flats available for boat fishing enthusiasts, and many of the inshore waters may be fished either by skiff or on foot.

The sight-fishing season on inshore flats begins in the latter part of May and continues through September. Beaches and off-shore flats begin a bit later, around mid-June, as fish move out to feed in these bigger waters through mid-September, when the fall migration draws them away.

This salt ponds and estuaries in this region offer numerous opportunities for inshore wade-fishermen. Excellent sight-fishing is found May through July in Rhode Island's Ninigret and Quonochontaug ponds. Prevailing southwesterly winds have carried beach sands across the barrier beach and into these salt ponds. This sand is deposited in the waters along the pond's southern shore, forming firm-bottom, white-sand flats. These are beautiful estuarine areas that have lush, tide marsh borders along much of their southern shorelines. The sand flats associated with these ponds serve as nurseries for several forage species, including grass shrimp, sand eels, silversides, green crabs and juvenile flounder in May and June. Later in the season, adult green crabs and silversides dominate the prey picture on the flats. Bottom-working patterns, especially Clouser Minnows, Del's Merkin (modified flounder-style) and green crab flies, work best through June. Later, both up- and down-style silverside patterns take the fish.

Many other inshore flats may be found along the south-eastern Connecticut shoreline. The areas associated with the

Southern New England offers countless inshore flats.

mouth of the Mystic River around Ram Island and along the western shore of Groton's Mumford Cove are two excellent inshore flats. Due to limited direct shoreline access, these areas are most often fished from a skiff, or are accessed by kayak or canoe and then fished on foot. These waters offer the same forage species as the Rhode Island salt ponds, and on the same general schedule.

The Narragannsett Bay shoreline in Rhode Island also offers this type of hybrid sight-fishing where inshore flats are routinely accessed by skiff. The western reaches of the bay yield sight-fishing opportunities as early as mid-May, and the fishing prevails well into the month of August. The bay is large (hundreds of square miles overall) and tidal flushing is ample which keeps these waters clean and relatively cool throughout the summer. Squid, sand eels and green crabs make up a good portion of the striper's spring diet in Narragansett Bay. Later, silversides, lady crabs and sometimes bunker hold the stripers' attention. The bay coastline is complex and unless you own a flats skiff and you're comfortable boating in these waters (there are several public boat launches throughout the upper bay), hiring a guide is strongly advised—there are some who specialize in sight-fishing.

Inshore flats available by boat are also found along the northern shore of Fisher's Island. Actually part of New York, Fisher's Island is a private island that is readily reached by boat from either Rhode Island or southeastern Connecticut. The north face of the island is protected from the surf and swell of Long Island Sound and is easily fished by posting-up the skiff. Several coves along the island shore sport smallish flats that run roughly parallel to the island and are often flanked by eelgrass beds. Fisher's Island is fabled for holding very large fish along its southern rocky shore, however, medium and large fish are typical on the northside flats.

Offshore sight-fishing is limited in this area, however, quality flats are located at the mouth of the Pawcatuck River, south of Sandy Point in Little Narragansett Bay and along the eastern reaches of the Connecticut River where it discharges into Long Island Sound. These flats, although not expansive, are large enough to accommodate multiple skiffs, either poling or staked out. Both areas are a quick boat ride from the neighboring mainland. Public boat-launch areas are located along each river. The bottoms in these areas are a shade darker than the white sands associated with Rhode Island beaches so to maximize your viewing I recommend fishing from the skiff for the added elevation. As is common with many offshore flats, spring and fall are the most consistent times to find stripers feeding on sand eels, silversides and crabs. In early fall, both the Connecticut and Pawcatuck rivers often hold good numbers of menhaden and herring making large up flies a very good pattern choice in September.

Rhode Island's southern shore consists of some of the most spectacular white sand beaches along the eastern seaboard—many are high-quality sight-fishing beaches. Excellent examples are Napatree Beach (west of Watch Hill), East Beach (east of Watch Hill), Scarborough State Beach in Narragansett, and East Matunuck. Block Island lies 10 miles off the coast of Rhode Island and offers excellent fishing along Grace's Cove and off Mansion Beach. Sight-fishing along these beaches begins about mid-June and prevails through September. Medium and large fish are common along these shores and the occasional whopper will have you sputtering for the rest of the day to anyone who will listen. Sand eels and shrimp are the main attraction through July along most Rhode Island beaches, followed by silversides and lady crabs through the end of September. Large up flies are always a good bet in September if there are any menhaden around what so ever. All of these beaches are readily accessed, however, during the peak bathing months of July and August, some beaches may not welcome anglers, some may have you parking a mile away, and some may be just too busy with the summer activity to be comfortably fished.

Public boat-launch areas include, but are not limited to, Ninigret and Qunonchontog ponds, Barn Island at the mouth of the Pawcatuck River, several marinas along either bank of the Pawcatuck near its mouth and from several

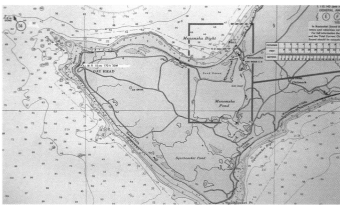

The west end of Martha's Vineyard offers excellent sight-fishing on inshore flats and in the surf.

public marinas accessible from Route 1A in Connecticut, between the towns of Stonington and Groton. The area in general has numerous hotels, motels and restaurants of all types, which greatly simplifies planning a trip to the area. All of these establishments, as well as several first-class tackle shops and guides (some specialize in sight-fishing) are available throughout the season.

The Rhode Island surf can have a tropical feel.

Martha's Vineyard, Massachusetts
(Lou Tabory)

Martha's Vineyard does not have large flats like Cape Cod Bay, Monomoy, and west and north sides of Nantucket. There is one better-size section of flats along the Island's northeast side, however there are good still sections of sight-fishing water and many small pockets. Like most of the Northeast sight-fishing, the Vineyard's flats are edges or shoreline strips, with some very good flats inside estuaries. We should call most of this "bar" fishing because I have had some of my best sight-fishing along the Vineyard's sandbars.

When looking at a chart of the Vineyard there are many good shorelines. Most charts do not show the second and third bars that exist along some beaches, or the bars protruding from the beach. I have had excellent sight-fishing on open-ocean beaches when the surf is down, drifting along in a boat keeping an easy cast from shore. Check these beaches on days of flat seas with offshore winds. The Vineyard has many such sight-fishing opportunities along light-colored sand beaches. Depending on the beach the fishing can be good at all tides. Ocean beaches, if you do not mind walking, are ideal for the shore angler and an offshore wind, which is the best time to fish them, and the casting is easy. The fishing might be productive all season as long as you have good overhead sun, but warm water will usually slow action, particularly on sheltered beaches.

With a boat on flat days, work the offshore shoals when the tide is slow. There are many shallow sections of sandy bars within several miles of the Island. Stripers will cruise the tops of these bars. Although this is not classic flats fishing, you will see the fish nosing along the bars, and sometimes they will lie right off the edges. At time of slack water look for fish to roam all over the shoals looking for food. Some of these shoals will have slow water for only a short while. Beware: fish the shoals only during times of low wind, and watch for large waves if the shoals are open to the sea. These shoals are treacherous and not for the novice boater.

There are also some good protected beaches and sections of shoreline that are not exposed to open water. Some of the beaches inside of bays and harbors will have fish. Look for fish in these areas on low incoming tide. On very flat beaches there might be action right through the tide. These beaches are actually better to fish while wading because you will spook fewer fish. Look for fish in two to three feet of water along any sand beach, even swimming beaches.

Martha's Vineyard offers excellent estuarine sight-fishing all season long.

There are many good flats up inside of estuaries, accessible for the shore angler, or anglers with canoes and kayaks. The walking angler can reach some good areas but anyone with a small craft can fish the entire estuary. There are many locations on the Vineyard that do not have shore access. Using a small craft will open up a host of quality places inaccessible to the walking angler. I prefer wading if the bottom is hard, using the craft to access the location. The estuaries can be hot in the spring with eager-feeding-fish fresh from the sea. This is the time to find big fish that are not as picky as they will be later in the season. If the water remains cool, and the traffic is light, sight-fishing can be good into midsummer in some of the bigger back waters. Mid-May to mid-July will have good beach fishing but during the high tourist season some places become busy, making fishing hectic.

I fish some very small sections of water, as well as the banks around the mouths of outlets that have cruising fish. I like to work small pockets and keep away from the crowds. The Vineyard is a very popular fly fishing destination and the bigger, well-known spots, at times, get heavy pressure. Do some searching, looking for small flats that have little activity from people. Something the size of a tennis court may have a constant flow of fish for several hours.

I have had my best success with sand eel patterns, but Jaime Boyle, an excellent Vineyard skiff-guide, uses a light-tan crab fly tied like a Merkin. Jamie uses crab flies that range in size from a quarter to a fifty-cent piece. Sand eels and spearing are important baits up inside the estuaries and along the sheltered beaches. Sand eels are the dominant bait on the ocean beaches and the shoals. I like sand eel flies one and one half to four inches long with lightweight eyes that let them slowly settle to the bottom. The lady or calico crab is the most important crab throughout the entire Cape. Look for green crabs over muddy or grass bottoms and around structure. Green crabs are more prevalent inside estuaries and along sheltered beaches but the calico crab is the abundant crab along most beaches. Look for small shrimp, one to one and one half inches long, inside the estuaries as well. You will find them on both sand and mud bottoms. A No. 4 light-tan bonefish fly is a good pattern to match the shrimp.

Mid-May to mid-June offers the best overhead sun and less-crowded conditions. The Vineyard gets an early run of fish, and depending on the weather from the first of May on can be hot. June to mid-July is usually the best time for bigger fish. Midsummer can be good, but some areas might have too much activity to allow the fish to settle down and feed. Fall can be good particularly on the shoals but the wind usually shuts these locations off to sight-fishing. The Island does offer many sheltered small flats that are good locations on windy days; wind can be troublesome when sight-fishing on the Vineyard.

Anglers who sight-fish the Vineyard must be content, at times, to work smaller waters. Pick a small secluded section of shallow clear water and hang tough; this Island has many hidden pieces of water still to be discovered.

Nantucket, Massachusetts
(Captain Jeff Heyer)

Mention flats fishing and most people conjure up images of Florida, the Bahamas, or other exotic tropical locations with bonefish, permit, and tarpon. Nantucket Flats consist of stretches of sand in the northeast Atlantic Ocean located about 30 miles south and east of Cape Cod. Not the most likely location for flats fishing, but due to the layout of the terrain, it proves to be some of the best available sight-casting for striped bass in the Northeast.

The Nantucket Flats are a series of sandbars and shoals with weed beds and channels that make up the Tuckernuck Bank. While this may not sound like much, it is surrounded on one side by Nantucket Sound and the other by the Atlantic Ocean. In the middle are Nantucket, Tuckernuck, and Muskeget islands. This combination of islands and shoals has created a vast area of contiguous bars that allow excellent shallow-water sight-fishing. These flats are generally fished from a boat, using a push pole to propel the boat around the flats as well as position the boat for the best presentation of the fly to the fish. Some of the flats are accessible from the shore at certain tides for wade fishermen. While our fishing season begins in late April to early May and continues into early November, optimal times for the flats are mid-June through early October.

While the stripers do not live on the flats, they, like most fish, are there to feed. Some of their dining choices include crabs, sand eels, silversides, mummichogs, and lobster. More often than not they are feeding on sand eels and crabs. For this reason we try to match flies that closely resemble these baits. Chartreuse/white and olive/white Clouser Minnows are always good choice and are almost always our first fly. Additional patterns that you should have available are variations of crabs, Deceivers, and epoxy sand eels. Most of the flies should be tied on size 1 to 2/0 hooks with variations in color and size. While the above flies are the regulars, do not be afraid to experiment. There are days when, no matter what you throw, the fish just won't eat. Do not get discouraged. Just

＊━━ ⟨◊⟩ ━━＊

The Nantucket flats.

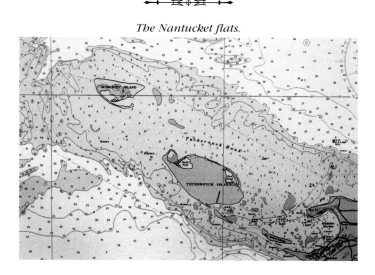

break into that fly box and pull out something else. One day comes to mind that proved this true. A client was getting rejection after rejection with the patterns he threw. After much frustration, he decided to try a different twist and tied on a large squid pattern. The fish went crazy and ate roughly six out of the next ten presentations. If I had not seen it, I truly would not have believed him.

The weather and tide have a lot to do with a successful day of fishing. As with most flats fishing, full sun and a light breeze are optimal. The tide is also important. Movement of the tide usually gives fish direction. Full high tends to be the most difficult tide to fish as the fish can spread out and not be as dependant on the bottom structure. This makes them more difficult to target.

Spotting striped bass can be as frustrating as spotting bonefish. One can be lying right in front of you and you won't see it until it swims away. Too late! The easiest method I recommend to someone new to the flats is to look for something that does not seem to belong there. Except during the extremes of the tide (flood high and dead low), water is constantly flowing. Stripers tend to move into the tide; everything else moves with the tide. Their movement is usually contrary to the normal rhythm of the water. Other features to key in on are the fish themselves and the shadows they create. When possible, always scan the entire area, not just one spot. Staring at one area not only limits your chances but also tends to lead to "mystery" fish. Never be fooled by dark spots on the bottom. Always check them out thoroughly before passing them up. There are several occasions when I wish I had cast to the "weed" laying on the bottom before it swam away. Once a fish is spotted never take your eyes off it. It only takes a second for it to magically disappear into the shadows and contours of the bottom. Like many creatures on earth, stripers tend to blend into the terrain. A fresh fish may have a dark back with very defined black lines. Once on the flats for a period of time, the colors fade and the fish becomes more silvery allowing it to better blend with the underlying sandy bottom. Their coloration may camouflage them better, but they still cast a shadow or silhouette so keep an eye out for it.

Our first choice in a fly line is a weight-forward intermediate, preferably clear. Besides aiding in limiting the spooking of fish, clear lines allow the use of a shorter leader on windy days. Floating lines are great and will work, but your hook up ratio may be much lower. For one, the tide is usually moving at a good pace, and two, the fish needs to see the fly. Even though you may be fishing in eighteen to thirty-six inches of water, the fish is focused on the bottom, not looking up. Intermediate lines and weighted flies make it that much easier for the fly to be in the striper's visual zone. After an intermediate line, my next choice would be a medium-fast sinking or sink-tip line. Again, you need to put the fly in the zone where the fish will see it.

As with most other forms of sight-fishing, casting plays an important role. Do you need to cast one hundred feet? Rarely! Do you need to be able to cast with accuracy? Almost always! If you can cast thirty to sixty feet with accuracy, you are going to get good legitimate shots at fish. That means leading the fish the appropriate distance for the conditions. How fast is the fish moving? What is the current doing? What direction and how fast is the boat moving in relation to the fish? All questions that have to be answered in a split second when deciding where to place the fly. Again, experiment! You can make the perfect cast and the fish won't eat. When this happens, hit him on the head. Yes, you read that right. Hit him on the head. Don't give any chance for the fish to recognize that it is not bait. You will get one of two responses. Either it will eat the fly or spook off. If you have made several good, well-placed casts and it did not eat, then spooking it off is not the end of the world. Most days you will get another chance.

While you can go out and be successful by yourself, odds are always better when you fish with someone else. This is true for a number of reasons. For one, more eyes mean more water is scanned making for better odds in spotting fish. Two, you need some control over the boat when presenting the fly. This is not easy when you are by yourself and you're concentrating on your cast and the fish.

Monomoy Islands, Chatham, Massachusetts
(Captain Kris Jop)

At the southeastern corner of Cape Cod, lies the town of Chatham. Over the years the quaint town has retained much of the flavor of the old Cape Cod. In just a quick boat ride from one of many public boat ramps here, fishermen can reach a sandy barrier composed of South and North Monomoy Islands. These islands are geographically situated in the middle of the striped bass and bluefish migration. Eleven square miles of a white-sandy bottom with average water depth of one to five feet creates a unique fishing destination. The sandbar structures and abundant shoreline around them practically guarantees that many fish will remain throughout the summer and into the fall to feed. Most of these flats are sheltered from both wind and the strong ocean currents, with the shallow water creating an excellent holding environment for all types of bait throughout the season.

Flats fishing on Monomoy is almost identical to that found in Florida or the Bahamas. The stripers and blues found here

Poling the Monomoy flats.

A beautiful Monomoy striper.

may not be as exotic as the species on subtropical flats, but their speed, strength and smarts satisfies the desires of almost any angler. The tackle and techniques used in this fishing are similar to those used to fish for bonefish, permit or tarpon. Like "Keys-style" fishing, it involves poling and sighting fish from an elevated platform. It's also highly recommended to wade these flats during the summer months, just as you would subtropical flats.

In large and complex areas such as those found around Monomoy, both high and low tide flats are present, offering good fishing opportunities at all tidal stages for those who have a boat and can move around. Remember that what may appear as an unassuming exposed sandbar at the low tide could turn into an ideal flat when the water returns with the incoming tide. This also applies to high tide where many good areas are invisible until the tide recedes.

One key to sight-fishing is the fisherman seeing the fish before the fish sees him or her. Accuracy and smooth presentation are also important. Placing the lure or fly into the path *in a non-spooking manner* is the key to success. An important factor to keep in mind is that flats and shallow waters have a distinct disadvantage for the fisherman in comparison to fishing deeper, structure-oriented waters. Stripers do get up on the flats to feed but often they are not behaving as

aggressively as they might in deeper waters. They are attracted to these flats because they perceive the lack of depth as a sort of refuge. In shallow water, the threat of attack by a predator diminishes significantly, thus allowing the free-swimming striper to focus on what surrounds them at their own level and above in water column. At times, they don't seem to be feeding at all, but are just passively cruising in the shallows. I call this "transferring fish" mode. Bluefish, normally warriors, also become wary foes once they venture into low-water locations. The slap of a fly, line or lure in calm shallow water will drive stripers and bluefish away to deeper locations.

The flats around Monomoy present great light-tackle and fly-fishing opportunities. The relatively high concentration of nutrients in the water supports intensive growth of the planktonic organisms like algae and members of the zooplankton groups. These organisms provide the base for the next level in the food chain represented by baitfish, crabs, shrimp and squid. The most abundant baitfish on flats are sand eels and silversides. From time to time, squid, tinker mackerel, juvenile herring and menhaden seek refuge there as well. When selecting flies or lures, spend a few minutes to determine which baitfish are present and make the appropriate selection by "matching the hatch".

The sediment on most of these flats is very rich in organic matter. This high concentration provides an ideal environment for marine benthic organisms like soft-shell clams, sea clams, nematodes and sea worms. During the months of May through October the flats around the Monomoy Islands are crowded with commercial shellfishermen. Using hand racks, they turn over the bottom sediment during the low tide on selective flats searching for clams. During this process, a relatively large amount of bottom is turned over to approximately two feet in depth. An incoming tide distributes loose sand and uncovers living organisms present in the sand and a natural chum slick is created. I have often witnessed schools of stripers maniacally waiting in the wash in several inches of water to enter flats so their feeding may begin.

Striper and bluefish feeding is regulated to a great extent by water temperature. The optimal water temperature range for these fish is between 56 and 68 degrees F. This temperature can generally be found around Monomoy from late May through July. In August, water temperature sometimes may reach 72°F but for the most part, it does not disturb stripers from coming on flats and feeding. Temperature returns to the ideal range again in September.

Fishing for stripers and blues in shallow water in the summer has traditionally been considered a nighttime or low-light activity. Daytime fishing on the Monomoy flats is a relatively new angling concept, but it is growing in popularity as more and more saltwater fishermen discover its challenge and excitement.

Sight-fishing from a shallow-draft boat has many advantages, especially if the boat has a poling platform. The elevated position enables anglers to spot fish more easily from a greater distance. A boat has the ability to cover more water on a given tide. However, around the low tide, I encourage my clients to wade the flats.

The flats of Monomoy have a relatively smooth sandy bottom with occasional grassy patches. The dark patches of eel grass are most abundant on the west side of the Monomoy Islands. If you are fishing there and not seeing fish it is still important to blind cast to these dark patches using preferably light color (white or yellow) flies. Stripers and bluefish like to use these grass beds as cover while waiting for the prey.

Wading is most productive one hour before and one hour after the low tide. The trip to a flat is made by a boat, then the anglers have a choice to fish from the boat or disembark and

The Block Island surf is very productive.

wade. The choice is influenced by the stage of the tide. When wading, we try to fish a particular portion of the flats and when these are explored a quick boat ride brings anglers to a new spot.

During June, as sand-eels congregate in the shallows to spawn, large (4-6 inches long) fly patterns work best. As summer progresses, the young eels emerge and begin to form large schools. Once you observe darker carpets of small sand eels on the flats, it is time to change fly imitations to smaller (2-3 inches long) sand eel patterns. In the fall months, larger patterns can be used again. Deceivers and Clousers in light tan and white imitating sand eels are consistent producers.

For the fly fisherman, eight- or nine-weight rods are preferable. For the best results I suggest using a Monocore line or the slime-line. Since it is practically invisible in the clear water, longer (8-12 feet long) and lighter (8- to 12-pound) leaders made from fluorocarbon are preferred.

The best time to fish Monomoy from the boat is the last three hours of the outgoing tide and the first three hours of the incoming tide. The combination of the low water and high sun yields the best visibility for sighting fish in clear shallow water. Stripers in the shallows tend to cruise on the bottom during the daylight hours so it is important to use a fly that will sink to their zone of sight as quickly as possible. The fly should also remain as deep as possible during the retrieve. Whether from a boat or wading, I find that fish that swim parallel approximately 60 to 100 feet from you are the easiest to fool. Usually, fish in schools are easier to catch because of their competitive nature, but sometimes single, particularly larger, stripers do not hesitate to strike a fly. When casting to a school of fish, try to aim for the lead fish on the edge of the school. If you spook a fish after the cast, simply let the fly sink to the bottom and begin the retrieve as soon as the following fish approaches.

As the tide ebbs, start looking for fish in deeper holes to set up their ambush positions. Stripers tend to hide or look for food in deeper channels, small holes or depressions on the flats. Baitfish like to hide in these spots too, and stripers seem to know that. Stripers also like to use the deeper channels as highways to move from one place to another. When they feel safe, they move into very shallow water in search of minnows, worms and crabs. They can often be found with their backs out of the water in as little as a few inches of water.

Once the tide has drained the flats, resume searching. You can often find fish stacked-up on the edges of the flats waiting for the tide to start flooding again. As the tide returns, the fish will follow it in search of sea worms, crabs and other types of food which become abundant at the sites where commercial clam diggers worked during the low tide.

Fishing around the full-moon tide is exceptional, because of the bigger tides. The increase in water movement often creates new fishable water because of greater depth fluctuations and stronger currents. Both incoming and outgoing tides produce action. An incoming tide draws inquisitive fish, which stop on the flooding flats looking for bait. An outgoing tide can also offer excellent fishing because the dropping water washes bait off the flats.

Before fishing in these and any unfamiliar areas, it is a good idea to check out the standard navigation charts for the Chatham area. It can help you to identify curves, dips and creases which define the routes that fish follow. It is important to note that on a chart, flats appear as large expanses of shallow water. The flats that were exposed during the low tide one year might be covered with water next year. Flats keep changing topographically every year, so you should also check the altered seascape at the beginning of each season to confirm their configuration and record changes on your charts.

Successful fishing in this area is not mastered in a day. I recommend making numerous visits to study the environment, enjoy the beautiful scenery and truly study the impact of the changing tides on this complex ecosystem. Taking these steps to discover Monomoy will enable you to more completely understand sight-fishing and to fully enjoy the thrill of landing your first striper here.

Cape Cod Bay, Massachusetts
(Captain Andrew Cummings)

A giant's arm, extending eastward and bending north at the elbow, Cape Cod reaches into the Atlantic from the Massachusetts mainland. A magnificent array of coastline waters surround the Cape—from the warmer island-strewn waters of Vineyard and Nantucket sounds leading way to the shifting sands of the Monomoys, jutting straight up the backside surf beaches, and finally, rounding the giant's fist, lies the north side—Cape Cod Bay.

A huge bowl, nestled on the inside of the Cape's arm, the Bay is somewhat sheltered from the southerly and easterly winds but very vulnerable to any weather approaching from the north or, more often than not, the west. It is these westerlies that dictate all activity of both fish and man on Cape Cod Bay. In addition to the threatening winds, the Bay's huge tides also play a vital role in limiting access to the water. Often reaching heights of almost 13 feet, the Bay's tides render most of the small shallow harbors dry for a period of time on either side of low water, preventing all boat traffic from entering or returning from the Bay. Although the combination of wind and tide on Cape Cod Bay creates a daily dilemma for mariners, these obstacles also help preserve and protect the Bay from over-exploitation by both commercial and recreational interests.

Historically, Cape Cod Bay has always been recognized as a deep-water fishery. Traditional trolling methods such as wire line jigging, umbrella rigs, and hootchies are practices and proven staples of the larger salon sportfishing charter boats. Over the decades, only a few anglers concentrated on the shoal waters of the Bay. There were two reasons for this lack of shallow-water interest: most conventional Northeast boats could not navigate in skinny water without running aground, and most tackle used was too heavy to make the delicate presentation often needed on the flats. Recent innovations in boat and tackle design have given anglers the opportunity to venture into the shallows and expand the diversity of the Cape Code Cod Bay fishery.

The shoal water that makes up the shallows of Cape Cod Bay are true hard-bottom flats, unlike the constantly shifting sands of most northeastern short water locales. The Bay's flats vary in make-up from hard-packed sand and gravel to huge expanses of eel grass. Due to the absence of rips or strong inlet currents, the contour of the Bay's bottom changes very little from season to season. Most of the shoal water in the Bay runs parallel to the shore, and in some areas, as far as five miles off shore.

In contrast to most striped bass inshore waters, Cape Cod Bay does not possess the physical structure or fast-moving water usually associated with the fishery. The angler pursuing stripers on the flats of the Bay must understand that wind and tide are the main force behind moving water, bass, and bait.

Due to the lack of structure in Cape Cod Bay, stripers in the flats tend to constantly be on the move, rarely staying in any specific area for any period of time. The angler must always be on the move as well which makes wade fishing difficult and often very dangerous. Without physical structure to concentrate fish, the wading angler must depend on sighting cruising bass. Height above the water is imperative for spotting moving stripers, and as a result, wading the flats creates a distinct disadvantage in contrast to the boat angler. The perils of wading Cape Cod Bay cannot be stressed enough. During low dropping water, anglers can wade over miles of tidal flats only to be faced with an incoming tide that has wrapped around the shoal, cutting the wader off from the shore. Early incoming water in the Bay rises at almost three feet per hour; an area on a flat that was dry during low tide may have up to six feet of water only two hours into coming water. Over the years, countless anglers have been injured or drowned in the Bay—a high price to pay for a fish. I urge anglers against wade-fishing in the Bay. If you plan to take to the flats on foot, please be sure to be equipped with emergency floatation gear.

A stealth approach is the key to sight-fishing the shallows of Cape Cod Bay by boat. The angler must always bear in mind

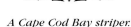

A Cape Cod Bay striper.

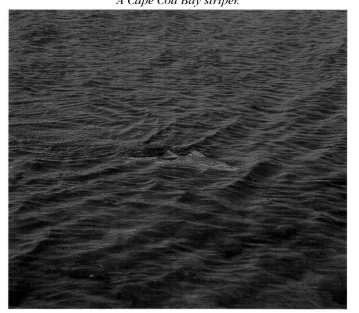

that the already wary striped bass becomes even more skittish in its behavior and sensitive to its surroundings while frequenting the flats. The boats best suited for shallow bay fishing are light skiffs in the sixteen- to twenty-foot length range; smaller crafts may be used, but are not recommended due to sudden increases in wind speed. The ideal Cape Cod Bay skiff has enough horsepower to allow decent range, has a shallow draft (less than one foot) and is light enough to be manually propelled or poled. Being able to pole the banks and shoals gives the angler a great advantage over the drifting boat. The ability to intercept and chase fish while creating minimal sound is crucial. Stripers are often found in bay flats water too skinny to use a trolling motor, and these small electrics are sluggish, causing difficulties staying with cruising bass. If poling a boat is not an option, drifting can also be effective. Because wind is the main force creating currents in Cape Cod Bay, and striped bass generally feed and swim against the current, a downwind drift will usually produce fish coming straight at the boat.

Some important ideas to keep in mind while sight-fishing Cape Cod Bay by boat: don't run over fish while under motor power; try to pole or drift to find fish; the less agitated the bass are, the more likely they are to eat. Give other anglers space and respect in the shallows; crowding just causes stripers to panic and bounce off one boat to another trying to get off the flat. If the outboard motor must be used to move on or near shoal water, please keep it at idle speed, and when leaving a flat under motor power, take the shortest, most direct line possible to deeper water. Think stealth and you will land more fish.

Cape Cod Bay's geographical location causes its water temperature to remain favorable for striped bass and a variety of bait throughout the season from May through October. Early in the season the depths of the Bay contain herring and mackerel; in mid-season squid keep the big bass busy; and bunker supply the forage for the late season. These larger baits can sometimes be found in the shallows but usually stay in the deeper water. In contrast, sand eels can always be found on the flats and big bass are caught in the shallows when other baits are scarce. It is always wise to be aware of what the offshore charter boats and commercial fishermen are doing; if their fishing is slow, the flats are often productive.

Sight-fishing the flats of Cape Cod Bay peaks and varies from year to year, but typically is productive from Memorial Day through Columbus Day. The larger stripers are usually targeted in the flats from late June through mid-September. In addition to sight-fishing stripers in the Bay, bluefish also frequent the shallows. In late May and early June, when the first of the sizable stripers arrive in the shoals they are often accompanied by slammer blues from 14 to 18 pounds. Smaller blues hold residence in the Bay throughout the summer months.

Throughout the season, Cape Cod Bay presents infinite opportunities for the sight-fishing angler. The Bay is incredibly inconsistent, yet never disappointing. Once you think you have the fish beaten, the winds shift and the bass switch gears—as must the people who pursue them.

Suggested Reading and Viewing

—*Stripers on the Fly*, Lou Tabory
    The Lyons Press, New York, 1999

—*Fly Fishing for Bonefish*, Dick Brown
    Lyons & Burford Publishers, New York, 1993

—*Bonefishing!: Your Passport to the World's Most Exciting Fly Fishing*, Randall Kaufmann
    Western Fisherman's Press, Portland, OR, 2000

—*Fishing the Flats*, Mark Sosin and Lefty Kreh
    Nick Lyons Books, Winchester Press
    New Century Publishers, Inc, Piscataway, NJ, 1983

—*Fly Fisherman's Guide to Atlantic Baitfish And Other Food Sources*, Alan Caolo
    Frank Amato Publications, Portland, OR, 1995

—*Permit on a Fly*, Jack Samson
    Stackpole Books, Mechanicsburg, PA, 1996

—Pop Fleyes, Ed Jaworowski and Bob Popovics
    Stackpole Books, Mechanicsburg, 2001

—*Saltwater Flies: Over 700 Of The Best*, Deke Meyer
    Frank Amato Publications, Portland, OR, 1995

—*Saltwater Fly Patterns*, Lefty Kreh
    The Lyons Press, New York, 1995

—*Practical Fishing Knots*, Lefty Kreh and Mark Sosin
    The Lyons Press, New York, 1991

—*Waves and Beaches*, Willard Bascom
    Anchor Press/Doubleday, 1980

—*Longer Fly Casting*, Lefty Kreh
    Lyons & Burford, New York, 1991

—*Advanced Fly Casting* (Video), Doug Swisher
    3M Scientific Anglers, Mastery Series

—*Northeast Saltwater Flyfishing* (Video), Captain Jeff Northrop
    Westport Outfitters, Westport, CT
    203-226-1915

Internet Marine Weather Netsites

Tide and Current Predictor
    http://tbone.biol.sc.edu/tide/sitesel.html

Atmospheric and Oceanographic Information
    http://www.fnoc.navy.mil/

Northeast Marine Weather
    http://www.narmar.com/storm.html

More Helpful Books for Fishing and Fly Tying

FEDERATION OF FLY FISHERS FLY PATTERN ENCYCLOPEDIA
Over 1600 of the Best Fly Patterns
Edited by Al & Gretchen Beatty

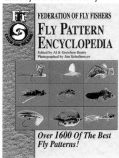

Simply stated, this book is a Federation of Fly Fishers' conclave taken to the next level, a level that allows the reader to enjoy the learning and sharing in the comfort of their own home. The flies, ideas, and techniques shared herein are from the "best of the best" demonstration fly tiers North America has to offer. The tiers are the famous as well as the unknown with one simple characteristic in common; they freely share their knowledge. Many of the unpublished patterns in this book contain materials, tips, tricks, or gems of information never before seen.

As you leaf through these pages, you will get from them just what you would if you spent time in the fly tying area at any FFF function. At such a show, if you dedicate time to observing the individual tiers, you can learn the information, tips, or tricks they are demonstrating. All of this knowledge can be found in *Federation of Fly Fishers Fly Pattern Encyclopedia* so get comfortable and get ready to improve upon your fly tying technique with the help of some of North America's best fly tiers. Full color, 8 1/2 x 11 inches, 232 pages.
SB: $39.95   **ISBN: 1-57188-208-1**

FLY FISHING AFOOT IN THE SURF ZONE
Ken Hanley

You'll find facts and advice on: Chum salmon, rockfish, cabezon, striped bass, surfperch, Pacific bonito, corbina, croaker, flatfish, sand bass, lingcod, and silver salmon; over 80 locations in Washington, Oregon, California, and Northern Baja; 21 fly patterns and full recipes, with angling tips for each fly; plus tips on equipment, water-reading skills, tides and moon phases, and field references for the traveler.

Ken Hanley is a pioneering spirit, with enthusiasm and excitement he shares his vast knowledge of Pacific Coast fly angling as only he can. You will get the insight you need to be a success at this "wild" game. 8 1/2 x 11 inches; 47 pages.
SB: $8.95   **ISBN: 1-57188-177-8**

FLY FISHERMAN'S GUIDE TO ATLANTIC BAITFISH & OTHER FOOD SOURCES
Alan Caolo

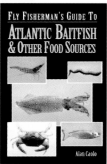

All the important baits from fish to crabs are shown large size and in full color, each fresh-caught specimen is shown in both top and side photographs. Included for each baitfish are: common names; distribution; seasons; predators; suggested styles and sizes of fly tying hooks; and suggested fly patterns, fishing techniques, and materials. You will return to this reference book again and again! 5 1/2 x 8 1/2 inches, 47 pages.
SB: $9.95
ISBN: 1-57188-017-8

SALTWATER FLIES: OVER 700 OF THE BEST
Deke Meyer

An all-color fly dictionary of the very best saltwater flies for inshore and ocean use. Effective flies for all saltwater game fish species. Photographed large, crisp and in true color by Jim Schollmeyer. Pattern recipes next to each fly. This is a magnificent book featuring the largest display of working saltwater fly patterns! 8 1/2 x 11 inches, 119 pages.
SB: $24.95   **ISBN: 1-57188-020-8**

VIRGINIA BLUE-RIBBON FLY FISHING GUIDE
Harry Murray

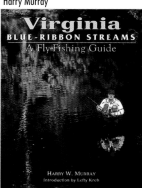

Virginia has a rich and vibrant history—President Hoover used to catch trout in the Blue Ridge Mountains to "wash his soul"—and a fishery to match it. The cool, clear waters of Virginia have much to offer the angler. Stream by stream, Harry Murray details their geography; the fish they hold; where and how to fish them; extensive resources; productive flies and presentations; and more. Virginia *is* for lovers—lovers of great angling in beautiful surroundings. 8 1/2 x 11 inches, 96 pages.
SB: $24.95   **ISBN: 1-57188-159-X**

INSHORE FLIES:
Best Contemporary Patterns from the Atlantic and Gulf Coasts
Jim Schollmeyer and Ted Leeson

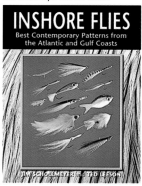

Inshore Flies is third in a series of three fly-pattern books created to introduce effective flies designed by knowledgeable local anglers and available in shops in a particular area—after all, no one knows better than these folks what patterns are most productive. Fly patterns are included for: New England states, Mid-Atlantic, Gulf states and Florida. Well-respected experts Jim and Ted collaborate once again to make this book a first-class project. 8 1/2 x 11 inches, 128 pages.
SPIRAL HB: $39.95   **ISBN: 1-57188-194-8**

THE FLY TIER'S BENCHSIDE REFERENCE TO TECHNIQUES AND DRESSING STYLES
Ted Leeson and Jim Schollmeyer

Printed in full color on top-quality paper, this book features over 3,000 color photographs and over 400,000 words describing and showing, step-by-step, hundreds of fly-tying techniques! Leeson and Schollmeyer have collaborated to produce this masterful volume which will be the standard fly-tying reference book for the entire trout-fishing world. Through enormous effort on their part they bring to all who love flies and fly fishing a wonderful compendium of fly-tying knowledge. Every fly tier should have this book in their library! All color, 8 1/2 by 11 inches, 464 pages, over 3,000 color photographs, index, hardbound with dust jacket.
HB: $100.00   **ISBN: 1-57188-126-3**

STRIPERS AND STREAMERS
Ray Bondorew

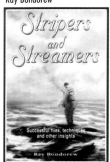

Introduction by Lefty Kreh
The striper is the ideal fish for the saltwater fly-rodder. In *Stripers and Streamers*, Bondorew shares his nearly forty years experience, giving us an in-depth look at what it takes to be a successful striped bass fly fisher, including: a history of both the sport and the fish, identifying the various water environs of stripers, proper presentations and flies, how paying special attention to the moon, wind, tides, current, and even the behaviors of birds and surfers, can provide clues to make you a well-informed striper fly fisher. *Stripers and Streamers* is the most up-to-date treatment of this fast-growing sport, with plenty for both beginner and expert alike! All-color, 5 1/2 x 8 1/2 inches, 120 pages.
SB: $19.95   **ISBN: 1-57188-072-0**

GUIDE TO SALTWATER FISHING KNOTS
Larry V. Notley

Saltwater fish have razor-sharp, bone-crushing teeth that can shred a leader, tippet, or knot in no time. Between their teeth and the enormous strength and speed of these fish, the use of well-constructed knots is a must. In this book, Notley shares 47 knots sure to keep fish on your line. With the same clear illustrations and instructions of his other knot books, Notley provides saltwater anglers with all the knots they need to keep fish on the line. 3 1/2 x 7 inches, 56 pages.
SB: $5.95   **ISBN: 1-57188-273-1**